I Promise.
REJOICE!

Carol Boseman Taylor

© 2015

Published in the United States by Nurturing Faith, Macon GA,
www.nurturingfaith.info

ISBN 978-1-938514-70-8

"Carol Boseman Taylor has been listening for the voice of God most of her adult life, and in this brilliant little devotional book she shows that she's heard it."

Jim Somerville
Senior Pastor, First Baptist Church, Richmond, Virginia

Carol Taylor has written a beautiful year-long conversation with God for personal devotion, Bible study, and spiritual growth. This is a book that you can read year after year and be challenged; comforted, and reformed. These conversations will truly let you hear the voice of God encouraging your personal journey towards deeper discipleship.

Bo Prosser
Coordinator of Organizational Relationships,
Cooperative Baptist Fellowship

"Carol Taylor's *I Promise. Rejoice!* is a different kind of devotional book. From the depth of her own devotional life and communion with God, Taylor dares to write from God's perspective. Rather than being based on stories or metaphors, both the title and the daily entries are written as direct words of comfort and challenge from God in the light of as-signed biblical texts for the day. Taylor's combination of empathy and insight offer a daring and meaningful approach to the enterprise of daily devotion."

Tony Cartledge
Professor of Old Testament, Campbell University Divinity School and
Contributing Editor, *Baptists Today*

"We are admonished on every side to pay attention, to listen, to be quiet, to find solitude, to wait on God. But it is not that easy. In our high-tech world, with multi-layer sounds, and doubled-booked calendars, it is more challenging than ever before. Carol Taylor helps us. Take her book every morning, find a special place to be quiet, then close that period of silence with a daily word from Carol and God. Listen . . . . . God's voice can still be heard!"

Linda McKinnish Bridges
Senior Director, Shorelight Education

I Promise. Rejoice! is dedicated to:

My husband, Charles E. (Chuck) Taylor, Jr.
You are my best friend and biggest cheerleader. Thank you for your unconditional love and for always encouraging me to reach outside of myself.

My daughter, Mary Blythe Taylor
You gave me the gift of being my "agent" for this book and encouraged me all along the way. Without you, I might not have had the courage to finish it.

My daughters, Anna Taylor Freeman and Erin Taylor Rice
Both of you share your love and encouragement with me daily. Your support and love are gifts beyond measure.

My friend, Pat Vess
You put "feet" to my even considering publishing this book. Your faith in me and your long-standing friendship are treasures from God.

My sister-in-law, Mimi Greenawalt Boseman
Had you not shared Wally Paton's book with our family, I might never have tried listening to God. You were the catalyst that got it all started, and you are truly a gift to our family. How blessed we are by you.

My sister-in-law, Janice Taylor Bobbitt
You asked for a copy of the notebook of readings and have been such an encouragement to me to move forward with publishing.

To each of you: I love you and am eternally grateful for your presence in my life and for your encouragement to me to get outside of my comfort zone and let God have his way with this book.

Life Guides

Carol Boseman Taylor is my friend and I am honored to tell you about her. Carol is a wife, mother, and grandmother; she is a Christian and friend to many; she is a leader, teacher, jewelry-maker, chef, prayer shawl designer and now, a published writer! Since 1986, I have had the privilege to know Carol. During that time, I have experienced her as a Christian who prays the Scriptures, an individual who takes time to listen to God and a woman who seeks to be spiritually formed. Most importantly, Carol Boseman Taylor is a person who yearns for God's direction in living life—practically and spiritually. Through her "real" life example and loving Christ-like spirit, Carol has effected change in this world. I know that she has made an impact on my life.

Now Carol shares her authenticity in this meaningful devotional work titled *I Promise. Rejoice!* She credits her writings as "messages from God" and describes her learnings as "holy offerings." Presenting a much needed communique, Carol's daily writings are concise, challenging and include Biblical references for your own "chewing" on the Scriptures. These devotions stem from Carol's experience of listening to God and journaling thoughts while encountering the world around her. Carol is true to who she is as an individual and characterizes her book as a life guide. *I Promise. Rejoice!* is truly an opportunity for practical application in listening to God, learning from God, and responding with God.

In her introduction, Carol Boseman Taylor posts a disclaimer when she writes that she is a "simple Believer, called to pray." A simple Believer, called by God to pray!" is exactly who I need in my life as a relevant example, a spiritual encourager, and a grace-filled petitioner. From Genesis 28:16, her July 4th devotional affirms that "Listening is essential" and "God waits!" Carol Boseman Taylor invites us to listen and wait for "Surely the presence of the Lord is in this place. Blotting out the noises of the world and listening for the sounds of nature I am ushered into the presence of God." I promise. Rejoice!

Ka'thy Gore Chappell
Winston-Salem, NC 2015

Isaiah 30:21: Whether you turn to the right or to the left, your ears will hear a voice behind you, saying, "This is the way; walk in it."

This book you hold in your hands seems to me to be more of a "life guide" than a devotional guide, but I will let you decide if it is so for you.

I am not a theological or Biblical scholar, nor do I hold advanced degrees in any field. I am a simple believer who has felt called to prayer and who has dedicated much of my time to journaling prayer requests.

For nearly 40 years, I have kept daily prayer journals. In them I wrote my prayers and offered them to God. It was really a list of "here is what I need from you, Father." For many of these years, I have used two devotional guides in my prayer time: *God Calling*, edited by A. J. Russell, and Jesus Calling, by Sarah Young.

About eight years ago, after reading a book called *How to Listen to God* by Wally Paton, I realized that it was time I stopped telling God what I needed from him and began listening for what he might be trying to say to me. I followed the guide outlined at the end of this book as I "listened" during my prayer times.

It was quite difficult to quiet my active mind as I sat with journal and pen in hand. Then, one day, something amazing happened! As I sat in a spirit of prayer, in front of a beautiful lake, words started to flow into my mind and through my pen onto the paper. The phrasing was quite unlike anything I might ordinarily say. The words were clearly not mine. This practice has continued—sometimes with more regularity than at other times. But the result is always the same: The words flow, and the message is something I really need to hear. It has felt like a "holy" experience and like sacred work.

The reason for calling this book a life guide is because its words are words of discipline, of teaching, of guidance, of comfort, of communion, of admonishment, and of love. Each time I read the daily offering, I am struck anew with how blessed I am to have received these words. The readings are true to the message of God's word.

It is my hope that these words will be a blessing to you.

Should you like to try listening to God, you may use the same listening instructions I used when I began this process. These words have been copied from Wally Paton's *How to Listen to God*.

Carol Boseman Taylor

Life Guide

JANUARY

1

Begin your walk through this New Year with the confident knowledge that I am with you. I will never leave you or forsake you. You can count on me, and that is truth.

Embrace the truth of my presence with you and allow the tensions to flow out of you. Rest in the knowledge that you are not alone.

Stop trying to figure out everything and listen to me as I share with you creative solutions to each challenge you encounter. Way will open in every case. I promise. Rejoice!

Proverbs 2:20; III John 1:2-4

2

Be still. Ignore the distractions. Listen as you go.

Pray, and in praying, believe. Why would I ignore your prayers? Do you not think that I, your God, have placed these concerns in your mind just so you will come to me? It is so. Nothing happens without my knowledge. What I desire from you is relationship, obedience, companionship, trust. The difficulties of life will be shared when you come to me.

Do not ever think that you alone can solve the problems of the world that I have created and of which I am aware. The burden is light when you trust and when you listen.

Why do you continue to forge ahead as if I am unaware of your trials? Why wait so long to return to trust? Why wait for desperate situations and desperate times?

I am bigger than your greatest problem. *I am* your God. I promise. Rejoice!

James 5:13-16; I Timothy 2:8

3

In this season of winter, look to me for your example of how to live. My trees have bare branches, but life (my life) still flows through them. The leaves that once adorned those branches now lie quietly protecting and warming the roots.

Do you see? I am always at work, even in the coldest, barest of times. Soon the spring will come, and the life (my life) will energize those same branches. Buds will form, and then the leaves. My world stands as a constant example of me. I am always present, even when you "feel" deserted. I am still there, working and waiting for the season of rebirth in your spirit. I promise. Rejoice!

Ecclesiastes 3:1; Titus 3:5

4

Gather with fellow believers and lift your prayers and concerns to me. You will feel my power more easily when you do this. Share each other's burdens, and in so doing your own burdens will become lighter and easier to bear. I mean for my children to bond together and to lean on each other. I did not create you to be alone. But always remember that just as you find pleasure and peace by sharing with others, these same feelings of pleasure and peace will be intensified when you make time to be with me.

I created you for companionship—with others and with me. That companionship is a part of your well-being—being "well" on this earth. Your companionship with me is vital to your "being well" (or to your "well-being") in a spiritual sense. Just as an earthly relationship needs nurturing, so does a spiritual one.

Opening up yourself to me and to others is important in so many ways—physical, mental and spiritual.

Come to me early and often, and you will be "heart-healthy." I promise. Rejoice!

Genesis 2:18; Philippians 2:1-2

5

Your truest friend—your best gift—is that of my son. Celebrate the Trinity in your life: Father, Son and Spirit.

Life without my presence is truly *not* life, but is instead merely existence.

Celebrate relationships because they (these relationships) all have a spiritual base.

Be kind. Be thoughtful. Be forgiving. Be compassionate. Be prayerful. Be *love*. Be "present" to all with whom you come in contact.

I am all these things and more in your life. I promise. Rejoice!

Ephesians 4:32; Philemon 1:5-7

6

These things amaze me…

It is not for you to understand *how* or *why*, even though your earthly ways thrust you toward these understandings. It is instead for you to *trust* and to develop your faith in me.

There will come a time when you will know and you will understand all things, but that time is not the present moment.

Can you still those raging questions? Those busy thoughts? That anger? That depression? That lack of faith and trust? With my help, you can.

Learn to sit quietly. Learn to allow my thoughts to permeate your mind. Your ego fights against it, but my spirit is stronger than all the earthly forces. I promise.

Remember my own exile, when temptations assailed me? You, too, can overcome these temptations. You *can* learn to just *be* in my presence. Practice the presence of God in your life. Each step of discipline you take brings you into my presence. Each tiny step builds on your relationship with me. I promise. Rejoice!

I Corinthians 13:12

7

Joyful, joyful, I adore thee…

And joy comes in the morning. When you can wake with a joyful heart, it is easier for my joy and peace to follow you all your days. Be open to joy. Be open to peace. Be open to developing a grateful heart. And in *all* things, give thanks.

I am a jealous God, and I am pleased to see my grateful, joyful children practicing joy and gratitude. It is contagious. When you go out and spread joy, others "catch the joy virus." Try it. You may be surprised. I promise. Rejoice!

I Kings 8:66; Psalm 100:2-5; Jonah 2:9

8

Be faithful. Set aside quiet time. Be still before me. Allow my words to flow through you. It is time for you to listen. Listen well. Record my words.

They are life-giving, encouraging words. They are instructions—and yes, even reprimands.

You need to set aside selfish thoughts and motives and listen for my still, small voice. "Hear" me through these written words. You will receive instructions. You must be faithful. I love you. I promise. Rejoice!

Jeremiah 30:2 (The Message); Mark 9:7

9

And the peace that passes understanding can be yours. I promise.

Do not let circumstances weigh you down. Do not let the bad attitudes of others block your ability to be positive. Circumstances and people will always be there, as stumbling blocks or as encouragers.

You must discipline yourself, through time spent with me, to follow the straight way. Do not lean to the left or to the right. Allow me to guide you and encourage you and love you. I am the *one* peaceful constant in this world. I promise. Rejoice!

Philippians 4:7; John 16:13; Isaiah 30:21

10

What time I am afraid…

Fear is not from me, child. Be confident of my love for you. Be assured that your times are in my hands. I am big enough to heal your hurting heart. I am competent enough to answer every prayer. Let go of your own expectations and plans and allow me to work my miracles in your life. I am able to do great things. I promise. Rejoice!

Joshua 1:9; Psalm 31:15; I John 4:18

11

You are called to pray, but lest you feel "puffed up" by this call, let me be quick to remind you that *all* my children are called to pray. This is my mechanism for communication with you. Be sensitive to your particular nudgings to pray. Be faithful. Be disciplined. But do not be proud. Pride is ego and ego is selfishness, and none of that is of me.

Pray. Listen. I am the one who hears and answers. I promise. Rejoice!

James 5:13-16; I Timothy 2:8

12

Beloved child, I know all that concerns you and all that awaits you. I have gone ahead of you to prepare a place for you. Think on these words as you go through each day. Consider them not only as what heaven is like, but as what heaven on earth is like.

I have prepared the way—rooms for you to inhabit—as you move through the moments and days of life.

Sometimes these "rooms" or places offer solace and comfort. Sometimes it is a room or a place of healing. It can be a place for joy and celebration, or a room of thanksgiving and gratitude.

Praise me for covering your life with my spirit. Give love and grace abundantly as you go, and it will return to you tenfold. I promise. Rejoice!

John 14:2-4

13

Sit quietly for a moment and absorb. Do not think on chores, nor worries, nor even your surroundings. Just absorb my presence.

I am always with you, but you are too easily distracted by the world— the sights, the sounds, the need to be busy, the desire to be where you are not or to do what you are not doing. Just relax. Absorb. Let my holy spirit wash over you like gentle waves. Listen for me. And then go forth, and I will lead you. I promise. Rejoice!

II Corinthians 3:18; Psalm 37:7

14

Do not become weary as you pray. Do not allow yourself to be discouraged when you think no answers are being granted to those prayers. Fear not.

I listen. I hear. I am working. I am answering those prayers.

Trust me. Trust me even when situations seem out of control and when things seem desolate. Trust me when you get frustrated at what you perceive to be no progress. Trust me on the dark days. Trust me.

I listen. I hear. I am working. I am answering your prayers. I promise. Rejoice!

Matthew 11:28; Galatians 6:9: Proverbs 3:5: Isaiah 12:2

15

Celebrate the day—no matter what day, no matter what comes your way. Celebrate the day.

Ask me how you should use these moments you are given. Follow my leadings for your life. Stay close to me. Be in tune to my leading you through this day, and celebrate. Find joy in the small things. Trust me moment by moment.

I am faithful to lead you through your moments. I promise. Celebrate and rejoice!

I Chronicles 16:27; Romans 15:13; Psalm 145:7

16

Do not let your hearts be filled with worry or anxiety about the days ahead. Face each new day with the calm assurance that I am with you, that I am protecting you, that I am the great physician, that I can provide for your every need. And be thankful.

Carry an attitude of thanksgiving wherever you go. Thank me in all things and for all circumstances. A thankful heart will lighten every load and bring joy and courage to others. I promise. Rejoice!

Matthew 6:25-34; Colossians 4:2: John 14:1

17

When you think you are fully engaged and listening for my words to you, take note of your body language. Are your shoulders tense? Is your spine rigid? Do you sense that your body is sending you a message that it is just waiting for you to finish this quiet time so that you can move on to the next activity? If so, just stop! Pay attention to those tense areas, and pray for an easing of that tension. Let the tension pass away, and then listen for my voice.

Holy rest I promise to you. Peace. You can face each moment with this peace if you will allow me to be present in you. Life goes on with its many difficult circumstances, but I am aware of each challenge and each joy. Treat each the same by relinquishing control to me. You will have a glimpse of my peace, which truly is beyond your understanding.

I am here with you, child, every moment. I promise. Rejoice!

Ecclesiastes 5:1-2; Mark 9:7b: Philippians 4:7

18

My child, you want life tied up in a nice, neat package. You want to be prepared for every circumstance and eventuality. Your desire is to control the world around you. You struggle with this because your spirit really does understand that you cannot be in control, but your humanness is confounded by this fact, this lack of control.

You glibly let the words "Let go and let God" slide off your tongue, but it must go deeper, and that fact must settle in your heart.

Trust me. Hope in me. Turn to me. Relinquish your idea of how things "should be" and allow my *spirit* to work in each and every circumstance.

It is not easy for you to do this. But if you will try, you will find your burdens and cares are so much lighter when you allow me to help you bear them.

I am here. I am hearing *all* your concerns. Write them down. I am listening. I am in control. *I am.* I promise. Rejoice!

Deuteronomy 1:32; II Kings 17:14; Psalm 9:10;
Nahum 1:7; Romans 15:13

19

There are times for action and there are times for quiet reflection. Be attuned to those times. Listen. Heed the impulses that move you in either direction. Ask me each day what I would have you do, and then follow. How else can you know the plans I have for you?

Obedience is a key in our relationship. You are prone to follow your own agenda, your own plans. I say to you: *Stop! Listen!* And you will receive guidance. I promise. Rejoice!

Deuteronomy 5:33; I Kings 8:58; Psalm 128:1;
II Corinthians 9:13; II John 1:6

20

Life as you know it is very much like the seasons you experience. There are cold, frozen times when I seem far removed from you and when you must depend on your memory of how I have worked in your life. I am not absent during these times, only dormant, and yet still working on your behalf.

Then comes the springtime, when you are able to listen and hear new truths and fresh insights. These are the times when you experience the most growth.

Times of summer are the lazy times in your life. You know me. You rest in me. But during these times, you are enjoying the fruit of what you have learned and are perhaps more inwardly focused.

And autumn? These are the times you use your gifts and your insights to store up treasures and serve others.

Life ebbs and flows. I have a plan, and that plan is for your benefit and for the good of others.

Stay focused. Contemplate how your own seasons of life are like those of nature that you observe.

Stay close to me and you will know my presence, sense my plan, and receive the instruction you need to follow my will for you. I promise. Rejoice!

Psalm 104:19; Jeremiah 8:7; Daniel 2:21; Jeremiah 29:11

21

If you can feel the power that sunshine has in your mood, your attitude, your life, then imagine how much more *son*-shine has—the presence of the Father, the Son and the Spirit.

Many of you suffer when you are deprived of the rays of the sun. That deficiency affects both your mental and your physical well-being.

Even so, the absence of turning to me, following me, leaning on me, listening for me, leaves you sadly deficient in spiritual well-being. And that spiritual health is even more vital in your life than the mental and physical health you seek so diligently.

Be diligent, child, about the time you spend with me. Be disciplined. When you do so, you will discover that the health that follows will be more complete, and that you will reap the rewards that come with a healthy, vibrant relationship with me.

What are these rewards? Peace. Joy. Love. Gratitude. Compassion. I promise. Rejoice!

Malachi 4:2; Matthew 13:43; Galatians 5:22-23

22

Turn to me when emotions and feelings seem to overwhelm you. I will bring balance back to your life.

In my world, all things have a point of equilibrium—a place of balance. That is part of the order which I have created.

When things go awry, it is because they are out of balance. Seek balance. Seek me. When you seek me, you will find me. I promise. Rejoice!

Deuteronomy 4:29-31; Job 25:2

23

Your loved ones are safe with me. When you pray, I hear, and I answer. Even when you do not have the words to form the prayers, I understand, and I hear, and I answer.

Do not become discouraged because you cannot see results. Just be faithful. Continue the conversation. Continue to communicate. When days seem darkest, I am still here. I still hear.

You must trust me. You must trust my timing. Just wait, though the waiting is hard, and believe. I am faithful to answer the prayers of my beloved children. I promise. Rejoice!

Psalm 9:10; Psalm 20:7; Proverbs 3:5-6

24

You must worship me in spirit and in truth. You need to acknowledge that I am God and I am spirit—Holy Spirit. The same spirit that is in me also dwells in you. I made it so.

When I created you, I breathed my spirit into you—into humankind. *This* is truth. So all you need to do, my child, is to recognize my spirit, acknowledge your *oneness* with me, and allow my spirit to work in your life.

What seems so complicated is really quite simple. Accept the truth that you, too, are spirit. Allow me to flow through you and out into the world you inhabit. If you will do this, there will be showers of blessing wherever you go. I promise. Rejoice!

John 4:23-24; Psalm 29:2

25

Praise God from whom all blessings flow. Praise and prayer are your watchwords for the days ahead. Each day, a clean slate awaits you. The past is behind, so do not look back.

Look forward and march steadily every day in the paths I open for you. Trust in me, and you will see my glorious answers to your prayers. I promise. Rejoice!

Deuteronomy 8:10; Isaiah 25:1; Romans 15:7; II Corinthians 1:3

26

After the cold and bitterness of winter, spring slips in with little fanfare until it reaches a glorious triumph. It brings with it renewal and hope.

So it is with your life. You experience dark and depressing times, but my spirit of springtime within you brings your own awakening and renewal.

Do not let your mind linger on the darkness of the past. Instead, focus on the breaking forth of spring, and give your heart permission to embrace hope and the glorious riot of color that is to come.

I was crucified on Friday—a dark and fearful day. But spring came on Sunday—a day of celebration for the bursting forth of eternal life, expressed in the confines of earth.

And so is my hope ready to burst forth for you and for your loved ones. Only believe. Practice believing. I am a faithful father. I promise. Rejoice!

Psalm 31:24; Romans 5:1-5

27

My children have a tendency to rush about, dashing to and fro. They seem to always be looking for the "next best thing."

What I want for you, however, is to slow the pace. I want you to experience the *now*. The now *is* the next best thing. Why? Because that is where you can find me. That is where our spirits join.

The journey is filled with lessons. These lessons serve to bring you closer to me. That is my deepest desire—to have us be and act as one, just as the Father, Son and Holy Spirit are one. Your deepest desire should also be to achieve oneness with me.

You try and fail and try and fail. Do not be discouraged. With each effort, you move closer to the goal. What you see as failure, I see as victory. It's true. I promise!

So see yourselves as victors in this life, and stride forward in new life. Rejoice!

Deuteronomy 2:7a; I John 5:4-5; Galatians 3:28

28

To God be the glory…

Praise and petition, gratitude and conversation, thanksgiving and love. I, too, am a grateful father. When my children take time to share with me, I am thankful. I created humankind primarily for communication with me.

There are rewards in a believer's life when this communication becomes a natural, necessary part of life.

Peace, joy, gentleness, sincerity, compassion, sensitivity, love—these are some of the rewards.

Situations ebb and flow. Personalities conflict. Hurts abound. Physical problems occur. All of that is part of life as you know it. But life as *I* know it is nothing like that.

When you spend time in communication with me, you begin to experience a bit of heaven and of eternity in your life. The best is yet to come. I promise. Rejoice!

Galatians 5:22-23; Ecclesiastes 3:11

29

When you feel that I am far away, stop. Read my word. Put aside your rampant thoughts and anxieties, and sit quietly before me. I am close. I am at hand. You need only to reach out to me. I can and I will bring peace into your lives.

You live busy lives, moving hither and yon, thinking ahead to the next thing. Your thoughts control your days.

I am not a God who wants you to rely on signs and wonders. I want you to trust. I want your steadfast belief that *I* am in control of your lives. I want your time and your attention, not out of duty but out of desire.

I love you and I need you. I created you for many things, and one of those things is companionship with me. I know you—inside and out. I know your needs and your desires. It is my desire to do good in your life. But first, *first*, you must stop. Stop the worries. Stop the frenzy. Practice quiet meditation. Practice being in my presence. When you can do this, you can truly become open to *my* desires for your lives, and you can watch in *wonder* the road *signs* for your lives. I promise. Rejoice!

Numbers 6:24-26; Mark 13:22-23

30

Do not be discouraged. I am with you. The things of the world can seem so desperate. The times in which you live can seem so desolate. But fear not. Put aside worry and bid anxiety to be gone. I am a loving father. I am a powerful God. All things can work together for good for those who know and follow me. I promise. Rejoice!

Hebrews 13:20-21; Mark 10:27

31

For the peace of God that passes all understanding is at hand for each of you. All you must do is *ask*, and you will receive. This is my promise to you.

This promise is not just for you, but for every person. When you pray, ask for this—for yourself and for others. I am able and I am willing to open this gift to you. With a peaceful heart, joy floods in. This peace—this joy—neither is based on your own feelings, attitudes or situations. They are gifts from the eternal one to each of you. Reach out your heart and receive my gifts. Your life will change. It will be a reflection of me. I promise. Rejoice!

Acts 10:36; Romans 15:13; I Corinthians 14:33; Philippians 4:7

Life Guide
FEBRUARY

1

All is well. I promise. I will sustain you. I will guide you and yours. Act on my promptings as if I were giving you a "to do" list. In fact, I am:

- Trust me
- Be kind
- Listen

I am speaking to you. I love you and those whom you love—even more than you love them. I am with you all. I promise. Rejoice!

Psalm 55:22; Isaiah 46:4

2

"Consider the lilies of the field." Look about you. What do you see? My natural world has responses to climate and to situations, but unlike you, they worry not. Built into them is a natural trust.

You, my child, have a choice: to trust, to have faith in me, or to trust and have faith in yourself and in this world of false truths. Which will you choose this day? For you must walk one step at a time. Choose one choice at a time. It is continual life, this life with me. How will you live today?

Choose me, and choose eternal life. It is there for the taking. I promise. Rejoice!

Matthew 6:25-34; Joshua 24:15

3

Lift up your eyes unto the heavens and open your heart to hear my voice—a voice that is not heard with earthly ears, but a voice that is heard through my spirit. Open your heart to me and release all your human feelings of hurt and anger. I will give you peace. I will give you direction. I will send you love and joy. I will be your provider—your guide and protector. *I am* your all. Claim it! I promise. Rejoice!

Isaiah 40:26; Isaiah 28:23

4

To God be the glory
Great things he hath done;
So loved he the world
That he gave us his son.[1]

To God be the glory, great things he hath done. Yes! Songwriters of the past listened to me and formed my insights into words for the ages to come. Read the words of hymns of old, and when you need a boost—a reminder that I am with you—go to the garden *alone* in the early part of the morning, and your day will reveal itself to you as I intend. I will "shower blessings" on my people. All you must do is be prepared to receive them and be aware of whence they come once they appear.

O God, my God, how majestic is your name in all the earth! I promise. Rejoice!

Psalm 126:3; Genesis 49:25

5

When you pray, turn over control to me. Do not pray hoping for your own agenda. Pray with wild abandon, waiting to see my answers—not yours. For you see, child, I have what is best in mind. You have good in mind—what *you* perceive as good. I have a deeper consideration. I seek to improve the whole rather than to "fix" a situation. I am the one who makes all things new. Wait and watch for miracles. If you wait, expecting, then you will see my answers slowly emerge. If you wait for your own answers to prayers, you will feel abandoned. Trust me. Love me. Have faith that I am working. Believe in me. And in my time, you will know your prayers have been answered. I promise. Rejoice!

Deuteronomy 4:7; I Thessalonians 5:16-18

6

The first step in overcoming any negative trait or emotion is recognition. When you can see with distaste the ugliness within yourself, you can come to me and lay it at my feet. My hope is that you can leave it and not try to reclaim it at another time.

Fill your heart—the empty places in your heart where the anger had resided—with love instead. Find good in those for whom you had anger. Pray for those people. Love them. Think about how I love all my children. Remember that those who have hurt you have also been hurt. Replace anger with love. Put aside hurt and replace it with love. You have no room—no time—for anger. It is not from me, but a product of your ego and your self. I am love. I will help you. I promise. Rejoice!

I John 2:1-2; Ephesians 4:26-27

7

Covered by my holy spirit, you move forward in this world you inhabit. Others see an earthly being, but I see a spiritual soul. My love and care go before you to prepare the way and are with you in each moment to enable you to follow my will. Trust me. Walk with me. Love me. And love others, thereby spreading my love as you go. I will never leave you. I promise. Rejoice!

Psalm 51:11; II Corinthians 13:14

8

The joy of the Lord is my strength… [2]

The joy of the Lord will overwhelm your soul, and you shall receive blessings that can hardly be contained in your heart. Believe me. Trust me. Love me. I am faithful to the promises I make to you and to your loved ones. I promise. Rejoice!

Nehemiah 8:10

9

Go forth fearlessly into this day. I am with you to help you. You have goals for the day, and I will help you. I have goals for you this day, and I need you to be attentive to me so that you can help me accomplish my goals as well. We are father and child. We are partners in this life. We are friends. But always remember that I am your God. All power and glory rest in me. But I am also a loving God, and my love flows through you. I promise. Rejoice!

Deuteronomy 33:26-27a; Luke 7:16; II Timothy1:14

10

Turn your eyes upon Jesus
Look full in his wonderful face
And the things of earth will grow strangely dim
In the light of his glory and grace.[3]

There are many "markers" in life—births, deaths, anniversaries—and they serve to remind of special events and special people.

What are the markers that remind you of me, your Heavenly Father? Are they memories of your choice to follow me? Are they memories of special times when you felt me close to you? I have markers, too. I sent my son. He was born. He died. I did all of this so that I could get your attention...so that you would turn your eyes to me. You are my children. I created you, and I love you. I am filled with joy when you recognize me and when you spend time with me.

I am your father. I am your protector. I am your holy friend. Turn from your earthly markers and mark time with me. Invest yourself in my kingdom's work. Pray. Love. Serve. And it will return to you tenfold. I promise. Rejoice!

I Thessalonians 3:6-7; Psalm 119:37

11

Tired...frustrated...anxious...

Fear not, little flock, for I am with you. I will comfort you and keep you safe. I am preparing the way before you. I am faithful to fulfill my promises to you. *I am.* What more do you need? What more can you ask? I am a parent who loves each child with a divine and eternal love. There is no heavenly reason for fear or frustration. I am here. I promise. And all is well. I promise. Rejoice!

Psalm 78:52-53a; Psalm 95:7; Isaiah 40:11; Luke 12:32

12

Lift your hearts as one to me, and I will hear and answer your prayers. Come together in a spirit of agreement, and you shall see my wondrous works. And as you pray, do so *believing* in me, *believing* that I will answer, and confident that you will see miracles in your lives.

Lean on me. I am strong enough. Believe in me. I am faithful to answer. I promise. Rejoice!

II Corinthians 1:11; Proverbs 3:5-6

13

Blessed are my children—each and every one of you. Even when the burdens of life weigh you down, when fears surround you, when disappointments overwhelm you, when illness shuts you down, remember: You are blessed!

You are blessed because you are *my* children. You are blessed because you know me. You are blessed because you have already received my gift of eternal life. The concerns you face in this life are nothing, *nothing*, when you compare them to the glories that are to come. I promise. Rejoice!

Deuteronomy 2:7a; Jeremiah 17:7-8; Matthew 5:6-12

14

The human element has created a day dedicated to honor and celebrate love. I have created an eternity to celebrate love. My love for you—and the love you have for each other—is a holy love, one designed to ease your heart and to bring you peace. My love is different than what the world celebrates. My love is all-encompassing. It is unselfish. It is giving. It is compassionate. There is no other love like my love for you. I promise. Rejoice!

So now, allow yourself to be wrapped in the warmth and comfort of my love—my presence— and find peace in this moment.

Deuteronomy 6:5-6; Jude 1:2; I Timothy 1:14

15

My children often try to solve their own problems without turning to me. Only when all fails do they ask for my help. But I say to you, take the easy route. Turn first to me. Ask and it will be granted you, seek and you will find your answers.

Your path could be easier, your climb less steep, if you only would first spend time with me.

Are you worried? Are you fretting? Are you anxious? Are you afraid? Are you distracted? Are you irritable? Are you disappointed? Have you forgotten to first spend time with me?

Seek me first, and I will be found by you. I promise. Rejoice!

Deuteronomy 5:32-33; Psalm 139:23-24; Philippians 4:6; Matthew 6:33

16

"Thank you, Lord, for saving my soul.
Thank you, Lord, for making me whole.
Thank you, Lord, for giving to me
Thy great salvation, so rich and free."

When the precious becomes ordinary—that is when your passion for Christ wanes.

When you look at the intricacy of a flower, you are amazed at its complexity. When you consider how a tiny seed becomes a massive tree, you cannot figure out how it happens. As you ponder these things, you have a sense of wonder. So, too, should you be amazed that the creator of this universe in which you live chooses to walk and talk with you—chooses to be your companion and your friend.

Do not let this precious gift become ordinary or too familiar. Approach my throne of grace with wonder and with a thankful heart.

Your salvation is no ordinary gift. It is a precious bestowing of eternal life. It is the gift above all gifts. Ponder this. Joy should fill your heart.

This gift is not given only for you. It is also for me. My love for you knows no bounds. I joy in our companionship. It is for this that you were created. Stay close to me. Embrace this gift. Wake with wonder each day—the wonder that your father in heaven loves you and desires your attention and your companionship.

This is an eternal gift for you. Unwrap this gift each day, and be comforted in my love. For I do love you, child. I promise. Rejoice!

Exodus 15:2; II Samuel 22:3; Isaiah 12:2-3; I Chronicles 16:34

17

When my children sit down to spend a few moments with me, it is often so difficult for them to focus, to be still.

It is like a young child who is being detained on the lap of an adult. The adult longs for the time to hug and cuddle the child, but the child is wiggling and trying to move away.

So it is with my children. Your minds wander and wiggle away, even if your bodies are still. You are thinking of things behind or ahead, wishing you had done something that you have forgotten or thinking of what you need to do.

You are no different than the child who longs to be off and running.

Practice stillness. Practice listening. Allow me time and space to hold you and hug you. Allow me the opportunity to spend time with you. It is your choice.

I made the choice when the world was created to form beings with whom I could commune. Won't you choose me this day? Will you practice being still and letting my spirit embrace you?

If you will do this, you will stand amazed in my presence. I promise. Rejoice!

Matthew 5:6; Psalm 46:10a

18

I know that you are often disappointed in your actions or your sins of complaining and of being critical, so I say to you, my child, turn to me before you speak. As soon as thoughts that do not honor me appear, turn from them and send a plea my way. I am ever present, and I will help you through those thoughts. I will replace those thoughts with thoughts of love and compassion.

Your words, then, will become a blessing to others, and you will feel lighter in spirit. I promise. Rejoice!

Job 15:5-6; Psalm 46:1

19

With God, all things are possible. Remember this! When concerns, troubles and frustrations seemingly block your way, remember that with me, all things are possible. Way opens.

Lay your concerns at my feet and truly I say to you, way will open. It may not be the way you expect, but you can trust and believe that I am going before you to clear obstacles and to make smooth your path.

Trust me. Listen for me. I will relay to you the proper path—the sure steps. You can count on me above all else. I promise. Rejoice!

Mark 10:27

20

Sit quietly in my presence. Allow thoughts to come and then release them, until your mind is open to listen to me. I will bring insight and wisdom.

Read my word. Heed my words to you. If you will do these things, blessings will flow over you, and joy, pure joy, will lift your soul. I promise. Rejoice!

Psalm 107:43; Proverbs 16:20

21

Though life has brought its challenges, I have brought you through them. I have heard your prayers, and I am still answering them. Be comforted by this fact. Stay close to me as you go through your days, and be attuned to *my* words to you as they enter your thoughts.

Stop if you must, and listen. And when you hear, then pray. I am guiding and directing and carrying you forward. Trust me. Pray to me. Be used by me. Believe in me. I am faithful. I promise. Rejoice!

Psalm 5:8; Proverbs 3:6, Proverbs 4:11-123

22

There are many who need your prayers, my child, many who are unable to lift their needs and hurts to me. I need intercessors for my children who are hurting and who feel so low they can no longer see the light of my presence.

Are you willing? Will you step into the gap? Will you allow yourself to serve me and others in this way?

You know through my answers that prayer changes hearts and attitudes. It can even change situations and lives. Do not treat this call to pray lightly. See it as your obligation, your responsibility, your divine calling.

If you will pray, I will answer. I promise. Rejoice!

Job 16:20-21

23

Any place I put you can be paradise. It is up to you. If you will think on me and my presence with you, then you will always reside in paradise. Heaven on earth. Heaven is "at hand." That means, my child, that it only remains for you to embrace me in all places and in all circumstances, and heaven is yours.

Claim it. Secure it every waking moment by living in each moment and trusting in me. I bring about the transformation in your life that makes your life divine and eternal regardless of your thoughts, your feelings or your circumstances. My children do not burn up in the fires of hell when they embrace me every moment. Instead, they live in glorious oblivion to the darkness and in recognition of the light of my presence.

What do you choose this day? Whom do you choose? Serve me. Love me. Trust me. I am faithful. I promise. Rejoice!

Psalm 16:8; Matthew 4:17; Matthew 5:3, 10

24

You reside in the middle of God's field. You are called to tend and to plant, and you are called to water, but only I, your Father and your God, can cause the growth. Prayer is the watering. Testimony, kindness, compassion, love and service are the planting. Do not think you are called to only one of these tasks. You are called to all. You are my earthly gardeners, but always remember that I am the master gardener.

So go forth and see my bidding with new eyes. Look afresh on the fields around you. Does the field need tending? Then prepare it for planting with love. Is the field furrowed already? Then sow your seeds of compassion and kindness. Are the seedlings popping up out of the ground? Then water with my spirit, which resides within you.

Prepare. Plant. Water. And I will bring the growth. I allow you to help me in this process to bless and grow you as well. Work my fields and watch for my blessings. There will be showers of blessed gifts on you—so much that you will be unable to contain them, just like a water barrel overflowing with the rain. I promise. Rejoice!

I Corinthians 3:5-9

25

My child,

...through broken toes and broken dreams and broken hearts

...through unmet expectations and unmet goals and seemingly unanswered prayers

...through lonely hearts and lonely lives and aching spirits

...through good intentions gone wrong

...in tries that failed

...through failing to live your best lives

...through these things and so much more—

I send you comfort, love and help, because truly you have no one else and nothing else and nowhere else to turn.

I am present
and faithful
and enduring
and compassionate
and loving...always.

For all of this, fall on your knees and confess your sins and cry out to me with a gratitude so deep you cannot fathom its beginning or its end. I am with you through it all. I promise. Rejoice!

Psalm 32:5; James 5:16; I John 1:9

26

Be faithful in the small things. Love. Send out love with every thought, with every action. Be my presence in this world. Let others recognize me in you. The rains come, the sun follows. That is the way with me. I cleanse and purify. I make things fresh and new. I send new joy, and I send hope. That is my way. Joy in it.

Surely goodness and mercy will follow you all the days of your life. I promise. Rejoice!

II Samuel 22:26-29; I Corinthians 1:9

27

Filled to overflowing. This is what I send your way. Acknowledge my presence, my "filling," even when I seem so far away—even when you are not proud of your own actions or thoughts or deeds. Practice my presence. Know that I am God and always near. Always.

I am near to your precious loved ones. I am with them. I am fulfilling my will for their lives as they allow me access to their hearts. I am giving rest and renewal to them all.

And as for you, be my friend. Let me lead you. Offer your heart as a sacrifice to me, and I will make your life a blessing. Trust. Have faith. Believe. Soak up the glory of the nature around you, and let me bless and revive.

Be very sure that I am God. I promise. Rejoice!

Genesis 12:2; Deuteronomy 28:8; Psalm 24:5; Psalm 128:1-4

28

In all things, see me. In all things, imitate me. In all situations, seek me. In all crises, know I am with you. In all—*I am.*

I am—Enough

I am—Love

I am—Plenty

I am—Conscience

I am—Grace

I am—Joy

I am—Healing

I am—Providing

I am—Always with you

I am—Lord

I am—the Great I Am.

I promise. Rejoice!

Leviticus 11:44-45; Revelation 1:8

29

Come to me, and you will find the rest you may not even know you need. I am all-sufficient. Do you understand what that means? I am enough. You may say it, but you need to believe it with all your heart. Come to me. My resources are *not* finite, but everlasting and abundant. I promise. Rejoice!

Matthew 11:28-30

Life Guide
MARCH

1

Why do I stay away from you so long, Lord?

Fear? Anger? Frustration? Are things not going "your way?" Then stop now and listen. Be still. Be quiet. Trust not in what *you* understand. Trust instead in me. I know all things, understand all things, and am in control of all things—especially of those things (fears) that occupy your deepest thoughts. Release those fears to me. Holding on to them causes you to be ill—not just physically, but spiritually.

Embrace me, and embrace wholeness and true health. True health has nothing to do with the physical and everything to do with the spiritual. Embrace me. Love me, and I will pour love out of you like a waterfall. It will be everflowing, like a fountain—sometimes rushing, sometimes quietly flowing. Trust me. I love you and yours, and I have all your circumstances—past, present and future—in my hands. Trust me. I am faithful. I promise. Rejoice!

Job 4:14; Psalm 3:6; Romans 8:15-17

2

O Lord my God, when I in awesome wonder
Consider all the worlds thy hands have made...[5]

O Lord, my Lord, how majestic is your name in all the earth. For your constant presence...for your love...for answered prayers...I thank you.

I will never leave you or forsake you, child. I am right here, close enough to touch, at hand. I hear your prayers. I answer them. I am your faithful father. I promise. Just believe! And rejoice!

Psalm 8:1; Psalm 48:1

3

Center yourself. Stop allowing your mind to jump hither and yon to all those things that inconvenience you. Put yourself aside. Once you have done so, my child, you have made space for me, your father and your friend. There is no one who longs more for your time and attention than I. There is no one who wants your friendship and love more than I. I promise. Rejoice!

Proverbs 18:24

4

Even when snow covers the ground and all of humanity feels cold and glum—even then, signals of my new life are appearing.

Look closely at nature. Crocus blooms show through the snow. Daffodils rise like sentinels as they prepare to bloom. Flowering shrubs' branches are nearly bursting with the possibilities ahead. So, too, should be the lives of my children.

Even though times are dark, dreary and sometimes fearful, you carry my life—my spirit—within you. That is a life filled with potential and possibilities for the times ahead.

Joy is coming. Peace is coming. Answers to prayer are flowing. Open the eyes of your heart and your soul, and you will see evidence of me and of my work all around you. I promise. Rejoice!

Job 37:6-7; Nehemiah 12:43

5

Clogged. My life is often clogged with situations, problems, to-do lists, over-active brainwork, responsibilities, and guilt.

There are some who say, "Let go and let God." Seems an easy and glib response to what all of humanity faces each day.

But there is truth in that sentiment. Truth is not always easy to embrace. You must be willing to relinquish something to gain my peace. That "something" is your time, your worries and frets.

Even in your busiest hours, should you voluntarily give up some of your precious time to sit before me, you would find that your remaining day will allow for all that is necessary.

You worry and fret, and yet, if you would sit at my feet, you soon would see those worries vanish. They would be replaced with my peace.

Nothing about what I offer you makes sense in a world geared to propulsion. But I say to you: Stop! Listen! Pray! Be present with me, and I will be present with you. Your life will become "unclogged," and you will find my peace and my joy. I promise. Rejoice! (Seek ye first.)

I Chronicles 16:27; Matthew 6:33-34; Psalm 50:14-15

6

Sometimes, I feel tired…irritable…anxious…disappointed…

You do realize, child, that what you describe are just "feelings," don't you? Feelings are (or can be) valid, but they are not permanent. They are not eternal. Truth is eternal.

Concentrate not on your feelings but on things that are good and on things that are true. Love, while some may call it a "feeling," is really a truth, an eternal thing. You cannot touch it, but it is there, and it manifests itself in so many ways.

Put aside your irritations and your fears and your disappointments and think on all that is good and true, and on all that is love.

You will find evidence of these truths wherever you look, in some of the most unexpected places. Why? Because those places are where you will find me. And I am love. I promise. Rejoice!

I John 1:6-7; II John 1:4; III John 1:4

7

Your anger at circumstances, situations and other people comes from a selfishness in your inner depths. You want to be in control, and when you cannot make people and life behave as you imagine and desire they should, the anger erupts. It is like a volcano inside of you, and most of the time you can hide the destructive fire and lava of your anger. You do not have the human ability to keep it always at bay.

This is a problem that humans (and that means *you*) must lay at my feet. I am the only one who can help you remove this monument to self that you try to hide.

You must daily, moment-by-moment, leave your need to control at my feet. Bring these ugly characteristics to me and leave them with me.

Trust me. Honor me. Love me enough to know that I can handle any problem. This may be one of the most difficult things you ever have to do, but you must do it. You must *die* to self every day. It is so hard, but it is the only way you can be open to the possibilities I have for you, for your concerns, and for this world.

Take note of all the irritations that bring to mind things you do not like—things with which you disagree. Imagine a bucket, and throw those thoughts in that bucket. Then bring that bucket to me and leave it. Walk away trusting.

At your innermost core, you must be able to trust my love, my compassion, and my abilities to handle your problems and your joy.

Give me all parts of your life, and you will find me able to care for you at every level. I promise. Rejoice!

Romans 2:8-11; Ephesians 4:22-24; I Peter 2:24

8

Child, I am with you, even to the ends of the earth. I will never leave you or forsake you. Your concerns are heard by me. Your way is charted before you. Do not fear. Do not worry. I am enough. I am love. I promise. Rejoice!

Deuteronomy 31:8

9

I know of your concerns for your loved ones. I know of your frustrations because you cannot yet *see* my answers to your constant prayers for them.

Have you considered that I do, indeed, have them in the palms of my hands? Have you thought that you, too, need to learn lessons? The lesson of faith, the lesson of letting go of your own solutions to problems, the lesson of trust? Believe in me. Trust me. Have faith that all *is* well and all will be well, for it is so. It is true. *I am* your Father and your God. I am beside you. I am with you. *I am.* I promise. Rejoice!

Matthew 8:26; Mark 5:34; Acts 3:16

10

I will never leave you or forsake you. You are my precious children. Your moments, your days, are important to me. Count on me. I will guide and direct your decisions and your steps. I am your faithful father and your friend. You can rest in me. I promise. Rejoice!

I Kings 8:57-60; Psalm 37:28a

11

It's not about me. (Jeremiah 29:11)

No child, it's about me. My spirit. My love. My presence. That is what I want my children to understand and to absorb.

It is about focusing on me and not on the circumstances of life. When I tell you I have plans for you—plans for a future and a hope—your finite minds rush to contemplate physical situations. Oh, how you miss the point!

All the obstacles and situations you face are not what life is about. No. Life is about how you respond to those things.

I give you new opportunities every day to learn to lean on me...to practice trusting me...to love me and others...to respond with gratitude and with thanksgiving, even when circumstances and situations seem hopeless.

Do not listen to the voices that try to say to you that I am setting up your life as if I am the chess master and you are the pawn. It is not so.

I give you opportunities and possibilities to follow my ways, to choose to hear my teachings for you and for the way you live your life. The choices are there for you. When you choose trust and gratitude and love, when you choose *me* rather than selfish pursuits, then and only then will peace and joy fill your lives. You will shine with the brilliance of my father. Others will know me, and most importantly for you, you will be at peace, regardless of what assails you. I promise. Rejoice!

12

In this world filled with angst and uncertainties, you can depend on me. You can trust that I am always near you—at hand—to protect and guide and direct you. All you need do is ask. I am here. I am faithful. I am your Father and your God.

Put aside worries for the future. Put aside your desires for material things. Put your trust in me, and all will be well. You will find contentment and peace if you heed my words. I promise. Rejoice!

Deuteronomy 7:9; Deuteronomy 32:4

13

My ways are not your ways, and my thoughts are not your thoughts. My plans are for the ultimate good for each of my children.

My love is stronger, sweeter and more encompassing than the love my children are capable of exhibiting. That is why you must continually be in prayer for me to love through you.

I know the plans I have for my own. I am at work in each life. Even when times seem darkest for you, the light of my presence is at work.

You fail to see my light sometimes, but it is still there. I promise. Rejoice!

II Chronicles 7:14; Jeremiah 29:11

14

May joy fill your heart this day. May you feel the love of God flowing through you and out into this world you inhabit. May you choose to be joyful. May you seek composure. May you sow love as if it were seeds of joy. Choose this day to put on my mantle of love, joy and compassion.

That is how each day should begin—with choices you make after spending time with me. Will life flow smoothly then? Not at all. But your spirit will have been renewed within you as a result of your choices, and you will know that I am with you. I promise. Rejoice!

Psalm 5:11; Psalm 19:8; Proverbs 10:28

15

Angry thoughts do not become my children, nor do angry words do anything to promote my kingdom. Let go of selfishness, because that is where anger takes root. Let go of self. Allow me to take over the space where self used to reside, and allow love to fill you.

Look to me to solve your problems and ease your frustrations. Turn to me for all things in every situation.

I will fill your hearts and lives with joy. I promise. Rejoice!

Matthew 6:33

16

O bless me now, my father…I come to thee.[6]

I am your morning and your night. I am your coming and your going. Take care, my child, to listen for my voice. Take care as to how you use your own voice. Even when you mean no harm, listen to me for permission to speak and to share. I am always attuned to your heart. You do not need to share your hurts and disappointments with anyone but me.

I know you, and I understand you. I created you. You must trust me more and rely on me more fully. You do not have to go to battle to right wrongs done to you or your loved ones. I see the hearts and the intentions of all. I know. I hear. I discern. I answer.

Let me be in charge. Just follow my lead. Listen more. Speak less. Wait for my guidance and my direction. I am ever and always with you. I promise. Rejoice!

Isaiah 40:1-2

17

Go about your day, doing ordinary chores, and the peace of God that is beyond understanding will descend upon you, and you will find joy in the mundane things of life. I promise. Rejoice!

Numbers 6:24-26

18

Distractions of the world can keep your spirit anxious and cause unrest within you. It is hard for my children to get beyond these distractions to spend time with me.

Ask me to quiet your soul. Petition me for all the things that make you troubled and anxious, and I will be faithful to answer you and to bring you peace.

First you must recognize that these distractions are separating us, and then you must ask. When you ask, I will answer. I promise. Rejoice!

I Chronicles 4:40a; Psalm 23:2-3

19

Just as the rains come down, washing and cleansing my world, so do I wash and cleanse you with my spirit. Open your hearts and your wills to me so that I may cleanse you and guide you into my truths and into my ways. Thereby will you know peace and joy. I promise. Rejoice!

Psalm 51:2

20

Trust in the Lord with all your heart and mind and soul. Trust is hard for my children because you want instant results. When you sense unanswered prayer, you take control. That is not trust. That is unbelief.

So trust. Even when years of prayers seem unanswered, you must trust. I am working, and I am winnowing out what is not helpful and what is not good in each situation and in each person. You must find peace in trusting, for you may never see the answers you hope for in your lifetime on this earth.

Rest in me. Trust me. Believe in me. Because, my child, I am faithful in all things. I promise. Rejoice!

Psalm 20:7; Proverbs 22:19

21

Go until I tell you to stop. Do not be afraid of the journey. Go with gratitude in your heart, remembering to be thankful each step of the way. Go in a spirit of joy and wonderment, amazed at what I can do in your life, in your journey. Go. Smile. Be thankful. Enjoy this journey with me. I am with you every step of the way. I promise. Rejoice!

Colossians 3:16-17

22

Examine my nature for evidence of renewal. The birds of the air, the waterfowl, the life around you celebrate my creation. So should you. Take time to listen and obey. Take time for me and for others. As you go forth today, practice putting others first. Take no thought for yourself and your own desires, but listen for my voice, my nudges, my guidance. You may very well receive a blessing.

Don't complain. My presence with you is my gift to you. Unwrap it each day. Be joyful. Be loving. Be mine. Because I love you. I promise. Rejoice!

Matthew 6:34; 7:12

23

Living water. Can you see it? The one thing everyone needs for life on this earth—water. The one thing everyone needs for eternal life with me is water. I am water—living water. I am eternal life. Drink deeply. Observe carefully. Floods, rains, ponds, rivers, seas. Living water. Sometimes stagnant, sometimes flowing, sometimes dead. Water. May you be refreshed this day by the water of my spirit. I am the source of all water and all life. I promise. Rejoice!

Ezekiel 47:9-12; John 4:11-14

24

You are learning. I am sending help along at each point when you need it. You do not have to fret or worry. I am with you. I am preparing the way even before your foot falls on a new spot of ground. I am there. Recognize my presence. Rest in me. I send you peace. I promise. Rejoice!

Matthew 11:10

25

Just breathe my name…

I am with you. I hear you. I love you. The things that concern you also concern me. Do not fret. Do not worry. Do not become obsessed with things you cannot change. Remember to show love. Walk with me. I will help you. I promise. Rejoice!

Breathe my name—Yahweh.

Jeremiah 30:2 — Write everything I tell you in a book. (The Message)

26

Write. Be open. Learn. Pray. Give. Share. Be hospitable. Care. Love. In so doing, you are accomplishing my work on this earth and in this place where you are planted.

I know the difficulties you face here. I am not unaware of your loneliness and pain. But can't you see how I have been and am still with you? You are not alone. In spite of all the things you perceive as difficulties, I am in the midst of it all. I will lead you out and on when the time is right. Do not fret. Do not fear. Relax in me, and let your joy and enthusiasm rush outward to touch the lives of others. Continue to be faithful in prayer. I will bring good to you and to your family. I promise. Rejoice! Amen.

II Corinthians 9:6; II Corinthians 13:11

27

Rest, my child. Listen for my voice in unexpected places. Do not think that you will live without conflict. Look at my life on earth. Through me you have the ability to *love* through conflict and unrest, if only you will keep your eyes and your heart focused on me. Do good to those who cross your path. Love the unlovely. Care for those who feel hopeless. They are all around you. Listen to the whispers of my spirit—my voice to you. Go about your life depending on me, and you will receive in return goodness, peace and joy beyond measure. I promise. Rejoice!

Deuteronomy 4:36; Isaiah 6:8

28

I am with you—that is truth and promise.

In your thoughts and cares, in the work of your heart and your hands, I am with you.

In your concerns for your family, in your foibles and your victories, I am with you. As you go, as you rest, I am with you.

I am greater than you can imagine. I am larger than your small being can fathom. I am that I am.

Just remember that I am in all. You cannot go where I am not. You cannot think but that I know your thoughts. You cannot act but that I know your actions.

Repent of wrong. Turn to me. Love me, for I love you. I promise. Rejoice!

Exodus 3:12a; Jude 1:24

29

For all these things I am thankful, Lord...

Remember to give thanks even when you do not "feel" thankful. Do not fret. Do not worry. Just remember (when these anxieties come your way) that I am with you—to protect and to guide. You are safe with me. Rest in that assurance. These are my promises. Rejoice!

I Chronicles 16:34; Psalm 100:4

30

Let me rest with you. Let me converse with you. Your lack of purpose is really my plan—a plan to talk with you. Will you make time to listen? Will you, in the coming days, sit at my feet? I have things to share. I have truths to give you. I need time alone with you. Do you not need time alone with me? Is that not the true test of relationship? Rest. Relax. Sit. Open your heart and your mind to me, and I will speak. I promise. Rejoice!

Jeremiah 29:10-14

31

This world has seen much. Read my word and you will know that people create their own problems. You do as well. Stop trying to make your will be done and begin even now to allow my will to work, life by life. You will see that I can and shall make a difference in this world. I still see hope on the horizon. I still love my people. I still care about each minute detail of every life. I have already conquered the evil of this world. Don't you remember? That battle is won! Only the unbeliever cannot see it. So trust and believe in me. Know with your spirit and your heart that all is well. All is safe. All is in my hands. I promise. Rejoice!

Psalm 119:105

Life Guide

APRIL

1

To what have I called you? You know that one thing for which I have tapped you is prayer—prayer for your family and for all the people and circumstances I bring to your mind. Yours is to listen and obey. Mine is to answer. I've already heard. I just want you to hear my nudging of your heart. Listen. Obey. The answer will follow. I promise. Rejoice!

Deuteronomy 4:7; Matthew 11:28-30

2

My child, listen and you will hear my voice in the everyday. Pause to fill yourself with me. Pray. I am waiting here for your attention. Come. You are weary and heavy-laden. In me you will find renewal and rest. I promise. Rejoice! Amen.

Psalm 5:3; Psalm 130:2

3

My child, abide. Rest your mind, and I will renew your spirit.

There are those who need your attention. Call them. There are those who need your love. Give freely. And there are those who need your prayers. Offer them to me.

I will ask nothing of you that I am not able to accomplish through you. Trust me. Be faithful to spend time with me. Be encouraged by my love for you and your family. Go forth this day in the knowledge that I am beside you and fully within you. Be not afraid, for fear is not from me. I promise. Rejoice!

Psalm 51:10: Matthew 10:8b; Matthew 10:28a

4

Have faith for your loved ones—all of them. I have them in the palm of my hand. I have promised you.

I love and guide them daily, and I will continue to do so. They will see my touch in the works of their hands. They will know that I am with them. Celebrate my presence in your lives.

Continue on a path to love and care for others as I bring them to you. Continue to be faithful to me, and in so doing you will be blessed beyond measure. I promise. Rejoice!

Matthew 15:28; Matthew 17:20; Matthew 21:21-22;
Deuteronomy 2:7; Proverbs 8:34-35

5

Listen. Slow down your mind. Stay focused on me and not on some "to do" list you have concocted. Do you not trust my faithfulness? Do you not trust my guidance? Do you not trust *me*?

If you trust, then be still, listen, and obey. I will not lead you where you expect to go, but truly I *will* lead you to glorious days you cannot yet imagine. So if you believe me, then why is it so hard for you to release your agenda and allow my blessings to enfold you? Why do you make life so difficult?

Just trust me. Believe me. Love me. And I will be faithful. I promise. Rejoice!

II Samuel 2:6; Jeremiah 7:23b

6

Why do I allow pettiness and anger to color my life? Why do I allow others to push my buttons? Why am I so unloving when those things happen? Why, Lord?

Oh, my child. The ways of this world are constantly trying to turn your heart from me. People who have withheld their spirit from me are desperately seeking to form their existence in their own way. You call them "control freaks." You allow their anger to infiltrate your spirit. Step back. Reflect on me. Love them. Release your need to control. Choose me. Choose love. If you ask me, I will help you. I promise. Rejoice!

Psalm 17:6-8; Numbers 14:18a

7

Here am I, Lord, sometimes unable to concentrate. Remembering the blessing of answered prayers...and how soon we can fall back into the old ways.

My child, be still. Your mind is racing but unfocused on my way. These days tend to distract and to depress, but being still and listening for my voice is the way. Be not discouraged. Be not afraid. Remember that this world has faced trouble many times. Trust me. Rely on me. Be assured that nothing happens without my knowledge. *I am* bigger than any problem. *I am.* I promise. Trust. Wait. Believe. Obey. Love. Listen. Rejoice!

Exodus 14:14; Psalm 37:7-11; Psalm 46:10

8

You are my child and you bring me joy, but still you have much to learn, much to overcome. In this season of newness, allow me to renew and refresh your spirit. As you see nature emerging from her sleep, know that you, too, can emerge from all that is dead within you. Allow me to surge through your spirit and bring new life to you as well. Let go of all the ways you try to exact control in your life and trust me to lead and mold. I am able. I promise. Rejoice!

Ruth 4:15a; Psalm 51:10; Isaiah 40:31

9

When I am running around (mentally), fretting, quiet me. Guide me. Comfort me. Protect me from myself and from outside influences, Lord.

My child, why do you wait to come to me? Why do you try to do things on your own? Your teeth are on edge, as is your very spirit. Stop. Release. Let it all go. Trust me to guide you. Trust me to lead. Trust me for your health and protection. Allow me to work my miracles around and through you. I am able to do all things, and you are able through me. Don't you believe? Can you trust? I love you and your family. I am faithful to provide. I promise. Rejoice!

Psalm 25:15-18, 20-21; Psalm 9:10; Proverbs 3:5-6

10

A season of promise: spring. Potential…new life…creativity at work for your loved ones and for you. I promise.

You have not yet seen nor have you acknowledged what I can do in your life and in the lives of others. I am the great *I Am.* I am a worker of miracles, the God of new life. I make all things new. I am full of surprises. Rejoice!

I Corinthians 2:9-10; Romans 6:4; Acts 5:20

11

Love surrounds you. When you fail to recognize it, it is because you have not opened your eyes to see. Life is not about "feeling" this love, it is about "knowing." Know that I am God. Know that I am love.

When you *know*, all is well. In spite of circumstances to the contrary, you can always *know* that all is well.

Pray for those whom you love. Pray for those who come to mind. Pray, and *know* that I will bring comfort and peace. Know that love extends to those for whom you pray, and that love begins and ends with me. Love abundantly through your own relationship with me. I am love. I promise. Rejoice!

Proverbs 3:3; Matthew 5:43-48; Matthew 6:5-15

12

And the glory of the Lord shone round about him…and it shines all around you as well.

Spring…a season of rebirth. A season that is of my design, intended to illustrate to my children the possibility of rebirth—the beauty of being born again.

You are indeed born again as my child, but you can also emerge from the darkness in your soul, from sin, from wrong choices, ill-chosen paths, even an immunity to my presence in your life. There is not only *one* rebirth. Take a look at nature. Rebirth happens over and over again.

How can you observe the world around you and fail to understand my pattern of forgiveness and my desire for renewal and rebirth? How can you not observe the beauty of my love and the intention I have of good for you? I have laid it out before you.

What appeared dead yet lives again. What was a small hard seed breaks open and grows into an amazing, productive organism. What was a branch pops out with leaves and blooms. It is miraculous. And so is my plan for you—my love for you. I promise. Rejoice!

John 3:3-8; Psalm 130:4; Acts 13:38

13

Surprises of joy await each of you when you allow me to be in control of your expectations. Leave all in my hands—*all*—and you will continuously be in awe of the life that unfolds before you.

You worry and fret about the things of this world. You allow your mind to work and work to figure out the hows and whys. Leave it to me. I can handle all things. You will be eternally surprised by my work in your life. I promise. Rejoice!

Matthew 6:25-34; Job 8:21; Psalm 5:11-12

14

I was faithful, though they slay me. Don't you think, child, that I understand what you go through? Don't you realize that my hurts were far worse than those you may endure?

I suffered insults and died on a cross. And yet, I was still faithful to my father. I did not waver. I did not spend time thinking how to retaliate or "get even." No. I asked, instead, for their forgiveness. I asked for my father's love to encompass them. I prayed for them.

Can you do less? Should you do less? Try today to pray for those who persecute you. Even if you see no discernible change. Even if you feel you get no results. Trust me to handle the situation. I am worthy of your trust. I promise. Rejoice!

John 19:17-18; Luke 23:32-34, 39-43

15

What do you take for granted in your life? Stop and consider *water*. It falls from the sky to nourish the earth. It flows and gains strength and power as it moves forward. It can be gentle and quiet, or rushing and powerful. It can be life-giving or life-destroying. It is cleansing, and yet it can be contaminated when it is misused. It contains life, and it nourishes life.

Consider how water can be like your relationship with me. There are so many lessons in life for you if you will only stop to consider. I promise. Rejoice!

Genesis 1:21-23; Psalm 1:3; Jeremiah 2:13; Revelation 7:17

16

"Break forth into joy…in the presence of the Lord, there is joy forevermore…"

Instead of contemplating the day ahead by listing your chores or appointments, by making a mental "to-do" list, try opening your heart to gratitude and thanksgiving.

Be grateful that you woke to a new day. Be grateful for the earth around you, for the seasons you are able to experience. Be thankful for the family and friends who fill and have filled your lives. Go forth with a thankful, grateful heart.

When you allow schedules, cares, disappointments or hurts to occupy your thoughts and mind, there is little room left for being thankful or grateful, or for joy.

It's a decision you make. Today. Will you choose the weight of the world or the light of my presence?

Choose this day whom you will serve. If you choose me, joy will fill your soul. I promise. Rejoice!

I Chronicles 28:9; Luke 4:8; Psalm 100:1-5; Isaiah 52:9

17

You must be born again. What does that mean for you? It means that you must put aside (behind you) all the past self-filled, self-focused moments, days and years, and start fresh.

Just as the spring breaks forth from seeming death, your spirit must seek a new, fresh start.

And you must seek me, and follow me, and choose me and my ways over your own self and your own selfish desires. If you do this, the freshness of my spirit will be with you always. I promise. Rejoice!

Acts 5:20; Romans 6:4-11

18

Lay out your concerns before me. Lay bare your soul. I know you, child. I know you inside and out, and yet do I love you. Though you feel disturbed in your spirit, I am sending you peace.

Let go of your anger and frustrations. Let go of needing to control your life. Let go, difficult though it may be, and allow my holy spirit to work within you.

Choose love. Choose to forgive. Choose generosity. Choose me and my faithfulness. Choose the higher road, and you will be blessed. I promise. Rejoice!

James 5:16; I John 1:9; Psalm 32:5

19

Eye has not seen nor ear heard what I have in store for you, my children. Continue to walk in faith, forward into your future, and mighty works and miracles will surprise you. I promise. Rejoice!

I Corinthians 2:9-10

20

Feelings sometimes arise within you that the world mocks you and is working against you. Face these feelings for what they are—lies and untruths. *I am* the truth, and I tell you that you should follow me, believe me. The unseen truths are what are real in this world. My spirit is real.

Trust in me to meet all your needs. Turn your back on false thinking, and turn your hearts to me. I am the truth and the life and the light of the world. Through me the impossible is possible. I promise. Rejoice!

Psalm 25:5; John 1:14; Matthew 5:14-16

21

Truly, truly I say to you that I am faithful in all situations and with each individual. Call on my name for every need, and I will respond. *I am* God. I can do all things. Do not let the world cause you to doubt or be anxious. Do not listen to negative voices. For *I am* the one who loves you and desires good for you. I promise. Rejoice!

John 14:13-14

22

Fear not. Though uncertainties seem to be following closely behind you, stay close to me, and I will stay close to you. I have made promises to be with you always, through good times and through bad times, through joy and through grief. Be assured that *I am* faithful to deliver on this. You have the assurance that *I am* already taking care of every detail that will cause you angst. I love my children and am here to care for your every concern. I promise. Rejoice!

I Chronicles 16:15; Acts 2:39; Romans 4:13

23

Cool breezes. Soft, dappled shade. Quiet waters. He leadeth me beside the still waters. He restoreth my soul.

The work I give you to do is not easy, my child, but the rewards are plenty. The peaceful settings, people who love you, my holy spirit—I send them your way. These are some of my blessings for you. Stay on my course. I will shed light along your way. I am faithful. I promise. Rejoice!

Psalm 23

24

In all things, give thanks. Develop gratitude for every person and every situation. Pray for positive thoughts and actions. Pray for my grace. Pray without ceasing. Gratitude and prayer can and will change your world. I promise. Rejoice!

Proverbs 22:11; John 1:16-17; Colossians 3:16-17

25

It is hard for my children to find zones of quiet, either in the world or in their own minds. Even when you sleep, there are dreams, and deep, restful sleep is often difficult to find.

You must try to sit quietly each day and allow the sounds and activity of the world around you to fade into the background. When you do this, you must ask me to help you still your active mind. This is harder for some than for others, but it can be done—with my help.

I need your attention. I need your quieted mind. I need your open and willing heart. For when you offer them to me, greater things than you can even imagine will unfold in your life. Taste and see that I am good... that I am God. I promise. Rejoice!

Psalm 34:8; I Thessalonians 4:10b-11a

26

When you turn to me, when you trust in me, when you let faith have free reign, then fear is frozen and my spirit is allowed to work unhampered. This is not easy, but with my help, it can be done. Turn. Trust. Have faith. Wonder-working power will follow. I promise. Rejoice!

Psalm 9:10; Psalm 20:7; Proverbs 3:5-6; Isaiah 12:2

27

I am the God of all seasons—fall, winter, spring and summer. I am the God of seasons of the heart and spirit—highs and lows, apathy and passion. I am present in each.

As you have times that are low, your tendency is to realize your great need for me. I joy in those times when you so ardently seek me. Just so, I want your gratitude and your thanks when things go well for you. I desire good for you, but I also desire communication with you.

Remember, my child, to spend time with me. Remember as you go, to stay close. When you can do this, you will feel my presence and my blessings. I promise. Rejoice!

II Corinthians 9:8; Exodus 33:14

28

Quiet. Peace. Wherever you go, whatever you do. That comes from *my* supply to you. Even when noise and worries try to enter in, I can supply these needs for you. Listen, my children, for my voice. Listen for my guidance and for my instructions to you. Continue, in your times with me, to lift the concerns on your hearts for others. This discipline is not for me, for I already know the needs. No, it is for you, so that you may learn to have compassion for others before yourselves. So obey. Listen. Heed. Love. I am always present to help you. I promise. Rejoice!

Leviticus 26:6; Numbers 6:26; Psalm 29:11

29

Shower love. As in a gentle shower of rain, let your love for others gently fall on all whom you meet. When you allow my love to flow through you, the blessings that come are multiplied.

Those whom you love are blessed, but the reflection of that love blesses you as well. So shower love wherever you go. Be filled with my love and my joy, and share with all, for by so doing, you fulfill my purposes for my children. I promise. Rejoice!

Isaiah 45:8; Mark 12:30-34

30

I am the way, the truth and the life. (John 14:6)

Turn to me. Talk with me. Make this your daily, even hourly, practice. All the "feelings" that seem to overwhelm you—fear, doubt, uncertainty, restlessness and more—are only just that: feelings.

The truth is that I am with you always. Every moment—waking or sleeping—I am ever present, always there. Your feelings are fickle. My presence is truth.

Put aside all negativity and worry. Put it behind you. Take my hand, and I will walk with you through all that is ahead. I promise. Rejoice!

Romans 10:10-11; Colossians 2:5; John 12:35-36

Life Guide
MAY

1

Father, forgive them, for they know not what they do. I said this, but you, too, should be able to say it. There are and there will be people in your life who hurt you and wrong you. You must turn these hurts and wrongs over to me, your Father in Heaven, and ask me to help you forgive them.

Replace the self-centered thoughts of hurt and anger and resentment with love and compassion. When it feels too difficult, ask me to forgive them, and then ask me to help *you* forgive. I am able. I promise. Rejoice!

II Chronicles 6:21; Psalm 79:9; Matthew 6:12-15

2

As life takes you to and fro…as you feel you are constantly on the move… as you seek times for quiet and reflection…turn to me. Ask me to help quiet your spirit. Find times when you can sit in my presence. Petition me to listen and to speak, and you, in turn, must also speak and listen.

Your active life and mind are distractions and hindrances to true, deep communication with me.

Ask and you shall receive. Seek and you shall find. It is so. I promise. Rejoice!

Jeremiah 42:3; Luke 11:9-10; Philippians 4:6-7

3

And I shall give you the desires of your heart, and when your heart seeks oneness with me, there shall be no leanness. My good and faithful servants shall experience goodness, pressed down and overflowing. Rejoice in these times. Wrap them in your minds as gifts. Share the reality of my goodness with others. The seeds you now sow will grow and bless you in years to come. I promise. Rejoice!

Psalm 20:4-5; Psalm 128:1-2

4

Truth = Safety + Security + Guidance
Victory = Brave and Trusting Heart
Rest in the presence (for there is the victory over evil)

Matthew 23:2-3: "The teachers of the law and the Pharisees sit in Moses' seat. So you must obey them and do everything they tell you. But do not do what they do, for they do not practice what they preach."

Blessed is he who comes in the name of the Lord. I promise. Rejoice!

5

There will be showers of blessings, and as you receive, then shall you give out showers of blessing to others.

This passage from my word is not about food, but it *is* about sharing love, joy, compassion, kindness, service, presence…meeting needs as God reveals those needs to you. Go forth, and do good to all you meet. Do as I command, and you will receive blessings beyond measure. I promise. Rejoice!

Matthew 14:17-21

6

Come unto me, child. I will rest your soul, and I will restore it. Why do you think you must handle everything yourself? Why do you square your jaw and set your teeth on edge? Don't you know all things are possible through me? Aren't you listening? Then hear me when I speak to you.

I am in control. *I will* be there for you. You need not fret or worry. You can do all things when you trust in me. Do you trust? Do you believe? This time is a test. The very ground you walk on seems so uncertain. Trust me to carry you. Trust me to guide you. Trust me to love you. Trust me with all your cares and concerns. Just trust. Why is that so difficult for you? Don't you know that I love you? Can't you *see* it with your spiritual eyes? I will free you if you will put your trust in me. I promise. Rejoice!

Numbers 12:6-8; Psalm 4:5-8; Psalm 9:10; Psalm 20:7

7

Fear not, little flock. I have promised to be with you. I have promised you eternal life. You know me. You sense my presence with you. Of what should you be afraid? Fear has no part of me. Trust me. Let my presence calm you. Let the knowledge that I am at work in the world—your world—bring calm trust to your life. Not just for today, but for all of the days.

Troubles assail you. That is inevitable because you live in a fallen world. But I can overcome those troubles. Do not focus on the negative—that brings on anxiety and fear. Do not fret. Instead, turn to me. I am *here* for you. I can overcome any problem in your life. I am joy and peace and love. Embrace my gifts to you. Embrace my presence. Let my light shine through your life on this earth. All is well. I promise. Rejoice!

Psalm 77:20; Luke 12:32; John 16:33

8

I come before you, my Father, with many concerns and thoughts swirling in my mind.

Quiet yourself in my presence, child. Be still before me. Be quiet. Be open. Be willing to listen. Only then am I able to enjoy communion with you.

There are many requests actively working within your spirit. Listen to me. Do not force your own will on any circumstance or desire. Wait for me. Do not run ahead of me. Do not push for your will to be realized. Instead, wait for me. I do not mean for you to do nothing. Proceed with what you feel you should do, but wait until I give you my approval. You will know my approval, my will, because resolutions will come in your life and into your circumstances with relative ease.

This is what I mean when I say "wait on the Lord." I can accomplish all things and so can you—through me. Always and only through me. I desire your companionship. I listen to your ideas, and I answer. Be sure to wait for my answer. Listen to the unease in your spirit. That is my "no." Listen to the sense of joy and forward movement and peace. That is my "yes."

You make life so complicated. Really, it can be a peaceful adventure if you will just let go of self and selfish motives and fear and, instead, trust me. I promise. Rejoice!

John 6:38-40; Psalm 5:3; Psalm 27:14; Isaiah 30:18; Romans 8:28

9

Where do your nudges come from? Those ideas and notions that come to you in the night? From me. Wait quietly. Listen to my still, small voice. I will guide you. I will lead you. There is a time of learning ahead for you, a time for you to turn to me and "hear" what I have to say to you with your spiritual ears. Fear not. This is not a time of punishment, but rather a sweet time of communion that I have planned for you. You will be refreshed and renewed. You will receive new energy and direction. Darkness will subside, and you will dwell in the warmth of my light. I am here. I am with you. I am never farther away from you than the length of an arm. You can reach out and feel my touch at any time. I am working for good in your life, for blessing. I hear and I answer. I promise. Rejoice!

Matthew 9:21-22; Matthew 5:13-16

10

You are being healed, my child. You are being healed—physically, mentally, emotionally, spiritually. You must believe me when I tell you this. You must embrace your healing. You must trust my touch in your life.

Your heart is downcast. That is resulting in many effects on your earthly body as well as your spiritual one. You must allow me to work. All I ask is that you become willing.

I can heal your lifetime hurts. I can heal the root of your problem. Let go of your need to respond to wrongs done to you. Let me. Let me heal you. You cannot change the heart of another. Each person has the ability to accept me or not. I am sorry, child, for the damage that has been done in your life. Choose love. Choose joy. Turn from the hurt. Discuss it not. Move on, and your heart will heal. Accept the love I am sending your way.

You can heal. You have the support system to do so. I promise. Rejoice!

Proverbs 16:24; Isaiah 58:8-9; Malachi 4:2

11

O Lord, my Lord, how majestic is your name in all the earth.[7]

Oh, my child, remember this: You need to make time for me. Time to rest. Time to absorb my joy. Time to know me better. Time to appreciate my world. Time to allow me to heal you. Time to appreciate my love for you. Remember: I need your time and your attention. It is so easy for my children to forget this simple fact. I need you to spend moments with me, and you need to as well. Rest in me. Be conscious of setting aside time for me. You will bless me, and you will be blessed by me. I promise. Rejoice!

Proverbs 16:32; Romans 12:12-21; Revelation 14:12

12

A busy day spreads out before you. You anticipate the events. Slow your active mind. Listen to the sounds of nature, which will remind you of my presence all around. Listen, learn and practice my love, my presence, living in the moment. It is here—in this moment—where peace is found. I promise. Rejoice!

I Chronicles 17:2; Ecclesiastes 9:7; Colossians 2:5

13

Strong, yet frail. You are wondrously made. Strong, to weather this world in which I have placed you, and frail, that you might recognize your need for me.

Come to me when your hearts are wounded, when you are hurting, when you feel frail, and I will give you rest.

Come to me also when you feel strong, when the world would say you do not need me. Oh, my child, how very much you do need me in those times. You must recognize that your strength comes from me.

You must learn to practice my presence at all times—good and bad—and learn to recognize me in all situations. My word reminds you of my closeness. I am ever present, ever close to you in all times, whether you feel frail or strong. I promise. Rejoice!

Psalm 139:7-18

14

Seek me and you will always find me. I am at hand. So near to you at all times, and yet you miss me so often. Stop. Look. Listen.

Stop your busyness. Look around you. Turn your ears to hear my voice.

Busy lives are one of the things that keep my children away from me. You get caught up in doing good, but you miss out on my best for you.

Busy lives prevent your stopping to observe my beauty that surrounds you. I have created a beautiful, even magical world in which you dwell. My spirit is in all things. I have made it easy for you to find me, but you are so involved in activities and thoughts that you fail to notice.

So stop the busyness. Look around you, and when you do, you will hear my still, small voice, speaking, directing, leading and communing with you. You will know my deep desire to communicate with you. You will know me. I promise. Rejoice!

Deuteronomy 4:29-31; Psalm 27:4-5; Exodus 33:13-14

15

On the days when you wake to the shining sun, it is easy to embrace me and believe in my wonder-working powers. Let it also be so on the gray, cloudy mornings when storms are close. Believe in me. Trust in me for your all. Leave behind worry and fret. Allow the breeze of my spirit to calm you and give you peace. All is well. All is well. I promise. Rejoice!

Judges 5:31b; Proverbs 4:18

16

Do you feel the tension in your body? Are you sitting in my presence just trying to "do the right thing" but already turning your mind toward the "next thing?"

Then sit quietly until you feel yourself relax. In that relaxed state, you will be ready to "hear" my voice and heed my words for you this day.

Practice coming to me daily, for just as people of old, you too need my "manna" each day. It is your sustenance. It gives you energy—spiritual energy—for your day and for the challenges you will face. When you invest in spending time with me, your dividends will return a thousand fold. I promise. Rejoice!

Psalm 107:43; Proverbs 16:20; Exodus 16:35

17

Let your hope be in me. Do not allow your thoughts (and your mind) to overcome the words I have for you. These are words of encouragement, of guidance, of peace and of love.

Walk forward in your life, ignoring the words of man that can pull you downward. Walk forward in the knowledge that you are loved, and that your Lord and your God is preparing the way before you.

I have gone before you in the past and have made the difficult times turn into blessings. Why would this time be any different? You are my beloved children. You seek my face, and I send you my love and peace.

Allow that peace to settle on you. Walk forward, listening for my voice. Act on my quiet commands. Blessings will come to you. You are under the shadow of my wings. Walk forward with confidence.

You will soon be amazed at my intercession on your behalf. I bless you, my children, this day and each day you live. I promise. Rejoice!

Psalm 25:5; Deuteronomy 5:33; Deuteronomy 4:33-40

18

And all the earth reaps the blessing of my bounteous beauty. Look around you in any season and you will be a witness to my handiwork. It surrounds you, from the changing skies to the earth itself. You are encompassed by magnificent creativity.

The same creativity with which I surround you is available to you if you will only embrace it. Whatever your circumstances or situation or location, I can help you create something beautiful—something meaningful. I promise. Just believe. Rejoice!

Genesis 1:1-5; Genesis 1:31

19

Love. Rest. Joy…in *me*. This is what you need. I promise. Rejoice!

Psalm 5:11; John 13:34-35; Acts 2:25-28

20

Blest be the tie that binds our hearts in Christian love. The fellowship of kindred minds is like to that above.[8]

It's true. Fellowship of like minds is a little like heaven on earth. Cherish times with like-minded folk. It does not mean agreement on all fronts, but a unified spirit of those things that matter most. Enjoy friendship and fellowship on this earthly plane and you will experience just a bit of what I feel when we share times together. I am love. Times with me produce love. So also do times of fellowship with believers. I promise. Rejoice!

I John 1:3-7; II Corinthians 13:14

21

For God so loved the world….
The world so needs your love, Father.

Natural disasters…human unkindness…disappointment of all kinds. Many things draw people to me. And if they are drawn to *me*, how can you think some things are all bad? I am big enough to ease the hurting hearts. I am strong enough to heal. I am loving enough for all eventualities. I promise. Rejoice!

Psalm 37:19; John 3:16

22

Standing in the need of prayer. Weak and weary. Troubled yet encouraged. Listening for your precious voice.

And I, child, have been waiting for you. Sit quietly before me, and wait. My love and my direction will come to you. My wisdom and peace will see you through. My strength will sustain you as you heal and as you help others to heal.

Fear not. I am always with you. I am protecting you and watching over you. I am using you to accomplish my work. Trust me. I am faithful. I promise. Rejoice!

Psalm 111:10; Exodus 15:2

23

Fear not, little flock, for fear is not from me. Fear is an invasive emotion that robs you of joy, of freedom, of hope. Fear is negative, and I, your Lord, am positive. I bring good; fear smacks of evil. How do *you* want to live your life? Do you want to be robbed of all good by such a negative emotion? Or do you want the joy of life with Christ to shine through you? Fear is *self*-related. Hope is *God*-related. Hope, hope, hope! Find joy in your life. Live a life based on thanksgiving. Live a life where you relinquish control of all to me. In so doing, you will find joy—not fear. I promise. Rejoice!

I John 4:18; II Timothy 1:7

24

The noise of the day already surrounds you. Your mind is actively processing the chores ahead. Though you set aside time for prayer and devotion, you are not allowing my presence active participation in your plans for the day. You are not finding a way to be grateful for each moment. Stop and let me into your moments. I can and will make a difference in how you see your day. I promise. Rejoice!

Colossians 3:16-17

25

Feelings of inadequacy nip at me...

Come to me when you are tired and heavy-laden, and I will give you peace.

This world is a troubled place, and troubles will always be found here. You desire a removal of those troubles, those problems. But I tell you that is not to be. In this world in which you live, you must navigate through your problems, and the lessons to be learned (and they are numerous) must be learned as you allow me to be the captain of your ship of life.

It is with my help that you can smoothly move through the rough seas of life. The storms will assail you, but I will sustain you. Turn to me as every wave rocks your lifeboat, and I will be faithful to steer your course. I promise. Rejoice!

Psalm 25:17; Psalm 34:17; II Corinthians 4:16-18

26

Going, going. Doing, doing. Seeking, seeking. Praying, praying, praying.

Always, troubles will assail you. The busy life will consume you. Doubts will follow you. Fear will leap ahead of you. Control will pursue you. But through it all, in the midst of it all, *I am*:

—waiting for you.

—loving you.

—seeking *you.*

—making the way straight for you.

—blessing you.

—protecting you.

—comforting you.

—calling you.

Come home to me. Come home to my loving, waiting arms. Come to me, for you are weak and buckling under the burden of life. I am here. I am at hand. I am waiting, child. Come to me.

I am here. I promise. Rejoice!

Matthew 11:28

27

Rid me, I pray, of selfish, self-serving, ungrateful thoughts and emotions.

Turn to me. Focus on me. In the shining light of my countenance, there is no room for self. Concentrate your thoughts and emotions on finding and doing my will. In that place, you will find joy and peace. Gladness will inhabit every corner of your being, and you will know closeness with your Heavenly Father unlike that of any earthly relationship. This, my child, I promise you. Rejoice!

Colossians 3:9-10; Matthew 5:48

28

Over-burdened…and yet grateful. Muddled thinking…and yet clearly aware of your presence. Thank you, Lord.

Wherever you are, you can always find me, because I am ever close at hand. All you must do is seal away the noise and activity and demands that surround and assail you, and wait quietly for me.

I will speak to you through my word and through my world. All you need do is listen. I will send thoughts to you. I am present. I am compassion. I am healing. I am encourager. I am love. *I am.*

I can meet any need you encounter. I can bring glorious victory to your life. Leave your troubles and concerns with me. Go forth with confidence and good cheer. Do not worry. I am with you in all things and in all ways. I promise. Rejoice!

Matthew 3:2; John 5:24-25; John 16:33

29

Oh, my Lord, how I celebrate the majesty of your name. When I consider the works of your hands, how can I ever doubt your love for me?

Oh, my child, I shower you with my love at every turn. Would you but notice, you would stand amazed at my presence, my influence in your life. I have no favorite children. All of you are loved by me. I have no agenda but to stand ready to love and guide you.

You must put aside worries and fretting. You must leave hurts and disappointments behind. Step aside now in the need to control each part of your life and allow me to be the one who guides and directs you. You can trust me. You can rest in the knowledge that I am faithful. Rest, and peace will flow through you, like a river. I promise. Rejoice!

Isaiah 48:18; Isaiah 66:12-13

30

Do not worry. Release your worries and anxious thoughts to me. They will soar away, and you shall have peace—my peace—which you cannot fathom, but which is more real than the hand with which you write my words.

Let your thoughts be positive. Walk in love. Do good to all you meet. And rest in the knowledge that all is well. Look not to circumstances as your gauge of what is right, but look to my spirit. I will not fail you. I hear. I answer. I am sufficient unto the day, the year. I am sufficient unto eternity. I promise. Rejoice!

II Corinthians 12:9-10

31

Waiting...I am waiting, Lord. Waiting for you to help rid me of thoughts and feelings that are unworthy of you and of me (your child).

Just rest in me. Sit quietly and allow my thoughts to inhabit your spirit.

Matthew 11:29-30

Life Guide
JUNE

1

Here I am, Lord.

As you sit waiting to hear my word for you, I entreat you to be quiet. For the day ahead will be filled with the busyness the world provides, but these few moments are for me and for you.

Peace be unto you. Peace as you abide. Peace as you stride. Peace as you pray. Peace as you toil. Peace as you go about the tasks that come your way. Peace and joy in your relationship with me and with others. Peace, blessed peace, I give to you, child. Worry not. Fret no more. I am the truth, the way, the life. I promise. Rejoice!

Psalm 29:11; Jude 1:2

2

This is the day the Lord has made. I will rejoice and be glad in it.

Help me quell anxious and irritable feelings. Help me today, Lord, to be more like you. I long to abide in circumstances that are not filled with petty tensions. I long to be able to be serene and at peace.

Your longings are heard and your prayers are answered. I know the needs and desires of your heart. I know you, my child, better than you know yourself. I am your creator—your father—your friend. You are safe with me. This I promise. Rejoice!

Philippians 4:6-7; Psalm 37:4

3

Darkness overcometh not. You must not embrace this darkness. You must allow me to help you overcome it. I can. I will. I must. You must release the hold it has on you. Do *not* revisit old hurts and worries. Do not labor among what you perceive to be your troubles. Look to the light. I have already sent you this subtle message: Swim toward the light. Do it now. Refocus your mind, and your heart will follow. I promise. Rejoice!

II Samuel 22:29-30; Isaiah 9:2; Luke 11:33-36

4

Fear not, little flock.

Worry and fretting do no good. Just pray. Trust. Things will not always go as you wish, but if you believe in me, then all will be well. I am able to be with you if only you believe. I am love. I am comfort. I am enough. Just remember that. I am enough.

Do you trust me? Practice that trust every moment, every day. And, in so practicing, you will see my face and hear my voice. I promise.

Genesis 26:24; Exodus 14:13a; Joshua 10:25

5

You are giving us rest and time for healing from a busy life. Thank you. You have given us beauty upon which to dwell. You have given us more than enough. I am so thankful.

My child, it is my eternal pleasure to provide beauty and peace. Would that you could always see and appreciate what is there in front of you, waiting to be savored and enjoyed. Would that your awareness of my presence were so keen that you recognized me in every moment of your day. I am here. Here for all my children. All you must do is recognize my presence. I promise. Rejoice!

Psalm 27:4-5; Isaiah 33:17

6

For the glory of your presence…for the beauty of this day…for your all-encompassing love…I thank you, Lord.

For what has been…for what is, and for what is to come…I thank and praise you, Lord.

Be still and quiet. Listen to the sounds of my world. Know that I am in control, in charge of all that you hear and all that you sense. There is a natural order in my world, and you are part of that world and part of that order. Why do you fret and worry? Enjoy the peace of the moment. Do not allow the manmade sounds and actions to turn your thoughts from me. Reflect on me. Think of a pool of water. You see a reflection there— not a complete picture—but then the water is disturbed, and though the reflection is also disturbed, it is still there. Whenever you look at that pool, think of me. Think of it as an example of how you never can fully appreciate the glory of my presence, but that I am always there. Just take time to gaze, and I will make myself known. I promise. Rejoice!

Job 25:2; Genesis 1:9; Leviticus 26:6a

7

For your overwhelming love, I thank you.
For your care for me, for my family, for others, I thank you.
For your provisions that ensure we have not only enough, but more than enough, I thank you.

Your life is changing, but I am always the same. Remember to make time for me. I am here, waiting for you at every crossroads, at every juncture, at every moment. At hand—within reach. In spite of distractions, I wait, ready to be with you. I want nothing so much as your love and your patient attention. Ignore noise. Ignore distractions. Ignore rampant thoughts. Wait on me. I am here. I promise. Rejoice!

Hebrews 6:17-20

8

"Turn Your Eyes Upon Jesus."⁹ Sometimes you feel far away from my presence, from my influence in your life. In those times, it is not *me* who is distant, but rather, it is *you*. You move toward the material, toward the busy chores in life, toward envy and the need for things and experiences. Move back to me. The spiritual experiences you will have in my presence are far more valuable than anything you can experience on earth.

Let go of your own goals and perceived needs, and allow my blessings to flow. Allow my spirit to move over and around you, and "the things of earth will grow strangely dim in the light of my glory and grace."9 I promise. Rejoice!

Leviticus 19:4; Numbers 6:24-26; Joshua 1:7; Acts 3:19

9

Unconditional love. Examples are all around you. If you have a dog (or have observed someone with a dog), you know the sheer joy it exhibits at your presence. If you have a relationship with me, then you should also recognize my pure pleasure when you choose to spend time with me. I am love. I am unconditional love. Seek to show this kind of love to all who cross your path. They will be blessed, and so will you. I promise. Rejoice!

Jude 1:20-22; I John 3:1, 16; Titus 3:4-7

10

My spirit waits for you. All you must do is sit quietly and invite me to join you. I am ever ready to fill your heart with my love and peace. I am anxious to send comfort to you. I am always at hand.

Listen, my child, for my voice. Within my words to you are admonitions and encouragements. You have much to learn in your time on this earth, but you also need to understand that I see your progress and am pleased when you follow my guidance.

You tend to see me as a father who admonishes and is ever unsatisfied with you. But, in truth, I am a "papa" who loves and celebrates each small step you take toward becoming the person I have created you to be.

Before the world was even created, I was love. Love created, and love endures. That is why *"I am." I am love* for you and for all. I promise. Rejoice!

Matthew 4:4; John 1:1; John 4:14

11

All is well. Though everything around you seems wrong and uncomfortable, all is well. You are fraught with the sense of unhappiness of others, but you are safe in my loving arms. All is well.

I have made you to be caring and loving and giving and sensitive to others. You need not take their despair as your own. Become, instead, a conduit from them to me. Lift their tears, which also fall from your own eyes, to me. I am father of all. I am here to handle the hurts and disappointments of life. You are standing in the gap.

I am allowing you to experience just a mite of the pain inhabiting the hearts of others. You could not bear it all. But I have borne it all. I can handle it, and I can love my children and help my children through their pain. I am enough. I promise. Rejoice!

12

Cast your troubles on my waters and watch them sink to the bottom and out of sight. Visual images can be understood by my children. Spiritual ones are more difficult. So use the visual images to "see" what I can do in your life—your spiritual life.

Imagine and then grasp my truths. I am God. I am able to handle your hurts and disappointments. I am there to celebrate your triumphs and victories. I promise. Rejoice!

Psalm 34:17

13

In the still of the morning, while the dew still rests on my world, sit quietly before me, and we will commune. Many seek times like this for a lifetime and leave our times together frustrated because they do not allow themselves to wait on me—to rest in me. Wait patiently for my words to enter your spirit. Listen carefully for the love I have to share with you. I delight in times of quiet with my children. I will never leave you alone. I promise. Rejoice!

Lamentations 3:22-23

14

Just as the rain refreshes the earth, so I refresh your spirit. The gentle rain-drops of my presence with you cleanse the sin, wash away the anger and resentment, and leave my sparkling spirit more visible in your life.

In life, you will face many emotions. Those emotions that do not honor me can be cleansed from your life when you take time for me. Remember these lessons. My world is full of lessons for you and for all who seek me and love me. I never leave you, nor will I ever forsake you. I am your Father and your God. I am here to teach, to chide, to comfort, to console, to love and to guide. Come to me, for with me there is no disappointment and no fear. I promise. Rejoice!

Jeremiah 31:25; Philemon 1:20

15

Noises of this world assail you, and you prefer quiet and the sounds of nature. But I say to you, child, that I am still present, still listening, still wanting you to choose to grow close to me. I am your Father and your God. Through me all things are made, and all comes to you. You inherit my riches. The riches you inherit from me are not what the world values. No. These are spiritual riches, with much depth and power. They are wealth for living your life and for doing my work. Open your heart and spirit to receive my riches—my blessings. When you do so, then you are empowered and enabled to go and to do in my name, and with my blessing, and with the power of the kingdom behind you. I promise. Rejoice!

Colossians 2:2-3; Ephesians 3:16-21

16

When you have time alone, how do you choose to spend it? Do you feel guilty if you are not sitting quietly at my feet? If this is true in your life, please put this guilt aside. I do want time alone with you each day. I want the best part of your day—the morning—when I have you fresh and ready to hear and receive my word, but I love your time whenever you choose to sit with me. In the evenings, it is good to close out the day with me. That will put thoughts of me into your subconscious, and you will allow me to work as you sleep. But I do not want you to feel guilty when you choose to do something that brings pleasure to you as you have time during the day. Just offer up the activity to me in silent prayer and you will have the comfort of knowing I am a part of this activity and I am with you, close by, in all that you do. I promise. Rejoice!

Psalm 23:2-3; I Peter 3:12; James 5:13-16

17

Worship the Lord in the beauty of his holiness. Holy, holy, holy...I am the Lord God Almighty. The times we spend in quiet are holy times for you as well. Look on your times of prayer and meditation as holy gifts. The communion we have is to be treasured. Leave these times with your spirit refreshed and renewed. When you are truly present with me, I am more able to shower you with the blessings of my spirit. You will experience me and know me at a deeper level. So come to me, my children. Sit with me. Talk with me. Listen to my stirrings in your heart. Receive my words, and share my love with others. The blessings you will receive will be beyond measure. I promise. Rejoice!

Psalm 29:2

18

No worries. No troubles. No frustrations. No cares. These are what my children desire.

But I tell you that you cannot live in the world without encountering those things. The worries, cares, frustrations and troubles will all be around you. *My* children, however, are called to turn to me when faced with these stumbling blocks. Turn to me, and give up these things that are troubling. Ask for my help. Pray. Then open your hearts and minds to be ready for the answers and solutions I send your way.

I am a creative God. I can lead you on paths you never thought possible. I can solve your problems in ways you never considered. Be open. Listen with a loving heart for my guidance. Be thankful. You are my children, and I love you. I desire good for you. But I will never force you to my ways. You must desire my guidance and leading in your lives. You must acknowledge my presence.

I am faithful to fulfill the desires of your heart. I promise. Rejoice! Only believe and be thankful!

Matthew 7:7-8

19

Surely the presence of the Lord is in this place.[10]

Signs. My children want "signs" of my presence. But I say to you, you should be always confident that I am with you. My word says when you seek me, you shall find me. That simply means that when you choose to be aware, sensitive, "tuned in," then you will find me. I am always present. Turn your heart and your thoughts toward me, and you will know beyond a shadow of a doubt that I am here.

No signs and wonders are necessary. I am here. I am present. I am listening. I am communicating. I am willing to walk with you every moment of every day. I promise. Believe! Rejoice!

John 4:48; Matthew 16:1-4

20

"For God so loved the world..."

Those words from my word hold a world of promise for my children. Phrased as they are, and with the verses following, they are meant to relay to each of you the depth, breadth, height and width of the love I have for you. You can only imagine in human terms the love I have for you.

By comparing my love to my son, Jesus, I hoped to illustrate what an amazing love you have at hand—a love that is really beyond your earthly imagination.

Think on this enormous love. Be grateful for it today and every day. And claim it as yours. Because, child, I love beyond measure. I promise. Rejoice!

John 3:16-21

21

Give me a compassionate and an understanding heart, I pray.

Have you ever observed the trusting love lavished by pets on their owners? Well, that is the sort of love I want you to have for each other. Once a pet has experienced kindness and love, it responds in kind with unconditional love.

You are called to be kind, compassionate, loving and understanding. To each one who crosses your path today, practice this. Put away your hurts of the past. Do not nurture ill will or grievances. Instead, I call you today to a loving walk with me.

With my help, you can show my love and compassion to others.

Sometimes it is hardest to walk this walk of love with family and friends. There is too much history of resentment built up within you. It is much easier to put on this "face" of love and caring to strangers.

I do not ask you to take the easy road. I ask, instead, that you climb the rocky path.

Go ye therefore to your walk this day, trusting me to enable you to take these first steps of kindness. As you practice my presence and set your mind toward kindness and compassion, your heart will follow. You will be amazed by the miracles that happen before your own eyes and within your own heart. For you must understand, my child, that this is the way

I have chosen for you. A way of love. A path of kindness. A highway of understanding and compassion.

Choose this day to follow my paths for you, and you can be sure you will never again walk alone. I promise. Rejoice!

John 13:34-38; Romans 12:10-21

22

What I want to do, I do not do...and what I do not want to do, I do. I am downtrodden, sad and disappointed in myself.

Put aside all thoughts of yourself—your failures and your triumphs. Do not feed on emotions. Instead, trust me to work in your life. Trust me to guide and direct. Trust me to comfort and console. Just trust me. In all ways, in all things, with all relationships, trust me.

I am worthy of your trust. I promise. Rejoice!

Romans 6:1-14; Romans 7:14-25

23

Be still and know that I am God. Let that thought sink in. Because, child, you seem to be anything *but* still. You seek me. You strive for faith to believe. I am answering your prayers and addressing your anxieties, but you spend so little time being still and listening for me. So today, practice this discipline.

That does not mean you should not engage in activity. What it means is that you should allow my spirit to have a presence with you, wherever you go and whatever you do. Let go of all anxious thoughts. Put aside frets and worries. Don't even allow the busy tasks to form a list in your mind. Just allow my words to become your thoughts as you go through this day.

Look for my blessings at every turn. Live today in gratitude and thanksgiving. Let me reign in your thoughts and mind today. Be still and know that I am God. Blessings will flow. I promise. Rejoice!

II Chronicles 20:17; Exodus 8:10; Deuteronomy 7:9; Psalm 46:10

24

You are being challenged to trust me, though you see no firm evidence that I am answering your prayers. You are being called to believe, though fears and anxieties appear at every turn. How will you respond to the challenge and the call?

Respond with joy. Respond with love. Respond with thanksgiving. Respond with gratitude. For I tell you that whosoever believes in me will be blessed beyond measure. Whosoever trusts in the light, when all they see is darkness, will be amazed at my wondrous works. Eye has not seen nor ear heard what I have in store for you. I promise. Rejoice!

Psalm 9:10; Psalm 13:5; Psalm 20:7-9; Romans 15:13

25

I put a song in your heart so that you will know my presence with you even when you sleep. I share thoughts with you on a spirit level. Stop over-thinking. Cease your striving. Let go of your need to know and to control. Allow my songs to be heard by your spirit and in your life. By so doing, my blessings will flow in and through you. I promise. Rejoice!

II Samuel 22:1-3; Psalm 28:7; Psalm 33:3

26

Build your house on a solid foundation. Build your life on my foundation.

When you listen to, and are moved by, the ways of the world, you are building your "house" (your life) on a foundation full of cracks. My foundation is firm and sure. It is unshakeable. You are safe with me. Choose this day whom you will serve.

Will you choose me, even when the world casts doubt on you and your plans? Will you choose me, even when the way seems dark and full of obstacles? Will you choose me?

Turn to me and not to the world. I am your faithful father and your friend. I promise. Rejoice!

Matthew 7:26-27; Joshua 24:15

27

Rejoice in all that surrounds you. Rejoice in good times and in difficult times. Rejoice in the relationships that make your life full. Rejoice, especially, that you are my child and that you have a relationship with me.

Rejoice and be glad. Look positively at the moments in your life. Enjoy them one-by-one. I bless you in the moment—in the present. Open your heart and mind to receive my many blessings. Do not allow negative thoughts to block your acknowledgement of these blessings. They are my gifts to you. I promise. And again I say, rejoice!

I Chronicles 16:10-11; Psalm 5:11; Isaiah 25:9;
II Corinthians 13:11-14; I Thessalonians 5:16-18

28

Though your life may have its "hot spots," the cooling breeze of my spirit is always wafting through your life. With it comes *joy*. With it comes a clear understanding that I am God, and I can do all things.

Much is ahead of you, but I am with you, and I am more than able to walk you through it—challenges, puzzles, mountain-top highs! I will be with you. I promise. Rejoice!

Psalm 147:18; II Timothy 4:22

29

You stand at the door and wait, but patiently waiting is hard for you. I ask you to stand firm and trust in me. I am faithful to answer your "door" and faithful to respond to your call. Trust.

As the parched earth awaits my rain, so does your parched soul await the refreshing of my spirit. Close your eyes. Praise me. Wait patiently for me. I am here. I am working for you. I promise. Rejoice!

Revelation 3:8; Revelation 3:20

30

I can do all things through God who strengthens me (Philippians 4:13).

You are "enabled," my child, to endure and to accomplish through my presence with you. It is when your spirit (your will) is connected to my spirit (my will) that marvelous things can happen in your life.

Taste and see the wonders that are ahead for you. Glorious times await you. Do not waver from the path I am laying out before you. Do not fear or "second-guess." Stay close to me. I am holding you close. Trust me, for I love you, and I am faithful. I promise. Rejoice!

Life Guide

JULY

1

Don't you know? Can you see? I am the father of miracles. I answer prayers. I cherish my children. I send you the desires of your heart. I do not ask much of you—just that you spend time with me, building trust, having faith, getting to know who *I am*. I know you, but I want you to know and love me as well. You are my creation—my masterpiece. You were not created in vain, but to have fellowship with me. You must seek my plan for your life. Stay in touch and in tune with me. Tap into the music of the universe I have created for you and you will "see" my face, you will "hear" my voice, and you will "know" my will. I promise. Rejoice!

Psalm 37:4; Psalm 139:14-17; Jeremiah 29:11

2

This is the day the Lord has made. Let us rejoice and be glad in it.

Tender are my feelings for the desires of your heart. Let those desires come into sync with my desires for you. Let my spirit guide your every thought, this day and every day. In so doing, you will see my hand in your circumstances and in your being.

My deep desire is to meet you and to commune with you. If you will open yourself to this—if you will prepare your heart and your mind for this—you will be astounded at what I can do in and through your life. I promise. Rejoice!

John 16:13-15

3

For the promises of this day
For my family
For all the people in my life
For the creature comforts
For the many blessings
For your love and care

Lord, I thank you.

And thanking me is enough, my child. I am eager to bless you beyond belief. I am eager to have you verbalize the prayers of your heart because I am eager to answer those prayers. I am happy when my children recognize that it is my desire to send good things their way.

Quiet...listening...lifting concerns...a thankful heart. These are things that bring me joy. Be open to me in your life. I stand at the door and wait for you. I promise. Rejoice!

Colossians 3:15; Colossians 4:2; Hebrews 12:28

4

Surely the presence of the Lord is in this place. Blotting out the noises of the world and listening for the sounds of nature, I am ushered into the presence of God.

As you await the beginning of each day, take time for me. Allow me to open the doors of peace and love and compassion and kindness to you. Allow yourself to sit and commune with me. Allow me to introduce to you the pleasures of friendship with me. Sit quietly and wait, and you will surely sense my presence with you. Speaking aloud is unnecessary. Listening is essential. I await your attention—your full attention. When you rest in me, I can commune with you. I promise. Rejoice!

Psalm 89:15; I Thessalonians 3:13

5

Thank you...for who you are and for what you are doing.

Trust me. Just trust. I am in the midst of life as you know it. I am present. I am loving my children. I am that I am. That means that in every relationship and in every circumstance, my presence *is*. Just recognize me. Have faith. Trust. Then and only then am I free to work. And after I allow you to see the work of my hands? Then praise should flow from your spirits. Be grateful. Be thankful, and let praises flow.

Our relationship is deepening and growing. Stay close to me and you will sense my presence close to you. I promise. Rejoice!

Nahum 1:7; Romans 5:13; Psalm 147:7

6

Busy though you are, my child, I am here with you, working out all your problems and confusion and waiting, waiting, for you to come to me.

Take this day and look for me. In the sounds and distractions, listen for my call to you to pray for others. In the quiet moments, listen to my leading and instructions to you. Listen. Follow. Be my faithful friend. I am here. I promise. Rejoice!

Proverbs 8:34-35; Deuteronomy 4:7; II Chronicles 6:21

7

We need a word for the people of God, Lord. A word of encouragement. A word of hope. A word to help us carry on.

Consider the lilies of the field, how they grow. All the words are there (in *my* word) for any circumstance and any situation.

My blessings still fall on willing hearts. My love awaits receiving. My presence hovers, awaiting recognition. Trust not on your own understanding. Turn from the ways of the world. Open the arms of your heart and your spirit to receive me and to receive the blessings I have for you. Listen with the ears of your heart to hear my bidding, my instruction, my guidance for you. Let the scales fall from your eyes—scales that prevent you from seeing me—and gaze at all I have in store for you.

I will give you the desires of your heart, but the desire of my heart is to love you and to communicate with you. If you will be open to me, I can do all things for you. I promise. Rejoice!

Matthew 6:28-34; Proverbs 3:5-6

8

Be not afraid. A spirit of fear should not abide in you, nor in the lives of your loved ones. I am here. I am aware. I am working. I am cognizant of your concerns and your problems. I see into the hearts of all, even those who seek to do their own will and follow the path of their own understanding, with no thought of me. Fear them not. For even though they bring momentary turmoil and discomfort, they are but a tiny aggravation in the face of my plans, a worrisome insect in my universe. Turn not to focus on their negative path. Keep your eyes on me and on the path I have for you. The companionship you need is mine. The approval you seek is from me. I am the only lasting, enduring truth in this world you inhabit. You are safe and secure in my hands. I promise. Rejoice!

Haggai 2:5b; John 1:14; I Corinthians 13:6; I Peter 1:22-25

9

Jeremiah 29:7-9: "Seek the peace and prosperity of the city to which I have carried you into exile. Pray to the Lord for it, because if it prospers, you too will prosper."

My children who seek my face will see it and will be astounded by my love for them. So seek my face. Put aside worries and pettiness that rain on you from those places where my light does not shine. Do not allow the darkness from the hearts of self-serving people to shadow the light I send your way. Turn from them and gaze on me. I bring good to you. I want good for you. I am your provider, not just of material things but also of spiritual bounty. Allow me to open my storehouse of goods for you. Stop. Listen. Pray. Believe. Do not be deceived. Open your spirit to me, and your life will receive blessing in abundance. I promise. Rejoice!

10

Thank you, Lord and Father, for all you do and all you are doing in my life and in the lives of my loved ones. I am so grateful to you and so thankful that you allow me to sense your presence and to "hear" your voice. To God be the glory!

Quiet rest is your instruction for this day. Put aside your own plans and allow me to guide your thoughts, your actions and your heart today.

Listen for words that can increase your understanding. Listen for my insight. Listen for direction for your life and for the lives of those whom you love. Listen for my admonitions to you. Listen for my wisdom. Listen to my world around you. Listen and learn. Listen and know. Listen and you will be comforted. I promise. Rejoice!

Mark 6:31; John 10:27-30

11

For the beauty of this earth that is laid out before me, I give you thanks, Lord.

Go in peace, child. Approach this day in peace, and I will be with you. Take comfort in my presence within and without. I am. I am *all* things. Nothing *is* but that it is me. I understand how hard that is to comprehend, but it is truth. Spirit is truth. Just listen. Just believe. Just trust. All is well. I promise. Rejoice!

Luke 8:48; John 4:24

12

My children, who are the creation of my hands, have within them the power to choose me. The hardships of life and of this world are not planned by me, but are the results of the choices of many. It is like a ripple on a pond that grows and grows—like a wave in the ocean that becomes larger and larger. When it hits someone and knocks them down, it is not a direct result of happenings and circumstances in that person's life, but it is the effect of many other happenings that have grown in magnitude as the wave moves toward the shore. You can be overturned in life by circumstances, or you can allow me to pick you up, dry you off, and set you firmly on your feet again.

And as that happens over and over again, you will learn to trust me. You will learn that I am with you always and in all things. You will become aware of my protective presence. When that happens, you will defy the ways of the world, and you will turn your eyes expectantly toward me. And you will wait—not with fear, but with hopeful anticipation—to see the pathway I have prepared for you. I promise. Rejoice!

Exodus 23:20-22; Proverbs 8:10-11; Psalm 16:11

13

For all the needs that you would have me lift to you, I pray.

Sometimes the cares of the world seem to be overwhelming. Sometimes the bad news brings my children down. But my view is a larger one. I see and know all things, and it is my desire to meet each of my children and to work in each life. When you feel overwhelmed, lay your cares at my feet. When you feel down, get down on your knees. When you have thought of an opportunity or of someone who needs me, just that instant you should lift that name or that situation up to me. I am waiting. I want to be asked. I await your call for help. I await your attention. I know the plans I have for you and for those concerns that are on your heart. I am here—at hand—awaiting you. When you seek me, you will find me. I promise. Rejoice!

Deuteronomy 11:12-15; Psalm 33:11; Jeremiah 29:11

14

The efforts you are expending in these days are tasks sent by me. You will not be sorry for the times you are experiencing. The memories and experiences of these days will become treasures. Trust me to work in all the situations of your life. Be thankful. Be grateful. Let that spirit of love and gratitude pervade every part of your life. You are my child, and in you I find pleasure. Be bold to speak out, but always be sure that your words are grounded in love. I am love. I promise. Rejoice!

Psalm 31:15-16; Jude 1:2; Jude 1:20-21

15

The reminders from your word and from your people call me to you, Lord.

Quietly, quietly, I bid you: Come to me. Come with heavy hearts. Come when there is joy. Come and rest in my presence. I am here for all times. I am found in all places. *I am.* Trust me with every moment of your day. Do not allow yourself to become so distracted with the events and problems you face that you forget to turn to me. Seek me in all things. I am faithful. I promise. Rejoice!

II Chronicles 7:14-15; Psalm 27:8

16

Seek me in the quiet of the morning as the chorus of birdsong escalates into the day. Seek me with spirit willing and heart and mind open to hear my words for you and to receive my love for you. Seek me always, and I will always be found by you. I promise.

Jeremiah 29:13; Amos 5:4

17

Your times are in my hands. You measure time in seconds, minutes, hours, days, weeks, months, years. But for me, time is irrelevant. I have no need for such measurements or such finite things. For you see, I deal in the infinite. Time-*less*-ness.

I see you as you will become. I have forgiven all that was, and I see you in eternity. That is so difficult for you to grasp. I understand that.

But you must release all those time burdens that you carry. Ask me to forgive all that is past, all that is *in* the past. And petition me for your future, for all that is ahead.

Ask me to guide you and direct your paths. Ask me to soften your hearts. Pray to me for love, for peace. Pray to put "self" behind you and to go forward with selflessness.

Pray, and I will answer. Seek me, and you will see that I am already here. Trust and believe, and you will begin to know me in a deeper, more personal way. I promise. Rejoice!

Psalm 31:15; I Kings 8:36b; Psalm 79:9; Psalm 119:35

18

Child, child. My deepest desire is to communicate with each of my children. When your chosen pattern of listening is interrupted, your lines of communication with me are still open. Do you not recognize that I have still been present? Have you not heard my voice in the voices of my children? Have you not felt my love through the care of others? I am here. I am always present. You cannot travel in either mind or space to a place where I cannot be found. Look around you and behold miracles great and small. Can you not perceive my presence? Every moment of every day, I can be found. I am at hand. Reach out for me, and you will be astounded at the nearness of my touch and the extent of my love for you. Think on the constancy of Christ, and you will be blessed. I promise. Rejoice!

Ruth 2:4b; Jeremiah 1:8; Jeremiah 29:14

19

Call forth joy and peace, Lord. Call forth promise and expectation.

My children reside in the palm of my hand. I am always protecting each of you. I bring love, joy and peace to you. I send others to you on my missions of mercy. Surely goodness and mercy will follow you all the days of your life, because I am with you. Always. I promise. Rejoice!

Praise be to the Father, the Son and the Holy Spirit. Amen.

Psalm 23:6

20

Help me deal with all the places where my heart is hardened, fearful and wounded, Lord.

Release the need to hold on to the burden of discouragement, the pain of past hurts, the anger of disappointments. Turn all of them over to me. Even if you must consciously release them over and over, continue to do so.

Each time negative thoughts come to mind, release them to me. As you practice this, also ask to have those vacant places, left by the removal of the negative, filled with love and joy and peace. In time you will be free, and you will be filled with thanksgiving at the peace that fills your soul. I promise. Rejoice!

Matthew 11:30; II John 1:3

21

Thank you, God, for this day!

Remember today that my love for you is all-encompassing. Remember the good that has happened in your life, and be grateful. Remember the challenges and how I have walked with you through each one, and be thankful. Rest with me today and know that I love you with an eternal love, and that all the days ahead will shine with the glory of my presence with you. I am always there by your side. I promise. Rejoice!

Jude 1:20-21; Mark 12:30-31

22

Anxiety, unrest, worry, frustration, concern. Call these by their true name: fear! Do not try to "pretty up" the truth with words. Fear is a lack of trust, a lack of faith. Have I not shown you that I, your Lord, can be trusted? Have I not demonstrated my faithfulness to you and to your loved ones? Believe on me. Trust in me. Live your life on a higher plain. Do not glance to the left or to the right. Instead, fix your gaze on me and walk confidently through each day. I am with you for every step. I am trustworthy. I am faithful. I promise. Rejoice! Believe in me!

I John 4:18; Proverbs 4:25-27

23

For the beauty of the days…for the peace of the night…for energy…for rest…thank me. Praise me. Depend on my goodness and my faithfulness. Be glad. Rejoice. Praise me always. Thank me continually.

I need to hear your voice as you also seek to hear mine. I am your Father and your God. Always. I promise. Rejoice!

Exodus 15:2; Luke 1:68; I Timothy 1:12

24

And let this be a sign unto you: Wherever you go, there you will also find me. I have not abandoned you. I will not abandon you. I send you signs that my joy and peace and comfort and protection follow wherever you are and in all of your circumstances. There is much ahead of you—much to experience—and I will walk each step with you. There will be times when your steps are slow and heavy; times when your feet feel as if they are dragging; times when your feet move you along confidently; and times when you skip for joy. I am with you, and I will be with you always. Fear not, little flock. I promise. Rejoice!

Deuteronomy 4:31; I John 1:7; Galatians 5:16

25

The only unchanging thing in your life is my love for you. Except for me, all things are changing.

There are seasons in nature and seasons in life. Change can be very uncomfortable for you, even difficult, but it can also bring blessings.

Think on nature, when new growth pops out in the spring and flowers of all colors appear. Think of autumn, when I paint a glorious palette on the trees just before the leaves fall to the ground to warm the roots for winter. Think of summer, when plants are fruitful and my children dine on the freshness and sweetness that life brings. Such are the lives of my children.

In all these changes, in all the seasons, look for me. For I am with you, even unto the ends of the earth. I promise. Rejoice!

Hebrews 6:17-20; Acts 14:17

26

Praise God, from whom all blessings flow. Praise him, all creatures here below. Praise him above, ye heavenly hosts. Praise Father, Son and Holy Ghost.[11]

Praise is good for your soul. Praise puts your thinking, intellectual mind on another plane—in a different dimension.

Praise is positive. It changes you and changes your focus. So praise me! When you are "up" and when you are "down," praise me. Remember me from days past. Remember blessings and answered prayers. Remember me, and remember that I am ever with you. I promise. Rejoice!

I Chronicles 16:12-14; Psalm 13:6

27

Just as a breeze rises from the humid stillness of the day, so does my holy spirit stir within you, bringing a freshness to your day, an awareness of my presence with you. Sit quietly for a moment and reflect on the refreshing of my presence with you before the day takes its opportunity to fill itself with busy thoughts and chores. Be still and know that I am God. Be still and allow me to embrace your life. Listen for my words to you. Let my thoughts fill your mind.

The quiet and the silence are your friends. There is no need to feel loneliness or emptiness or despair, for I am here—at hand. I promise. Rejoice!

John 14:26-27; Mark 6:31; Proverbs 17:1

28

Holy ground. You are on holy ground. Whenever you come into my presence (regardless of *where* you are), you are on holy ground.

Being my child requires practice and discipline. Yes, you have acknowledged me. Yes, you have embraced me. But my desire is to spend time with you. My desire is for you to so frequently practice my presence with you that it comes as naturally as taking your next breath.

Breathe in. Breathe out. I am here. Breathe in. Breathe out. I am always with you. I am so much a part of you that our spirits seem as one. When this happens in your life, great things will follow. Prayers will be answered. Miracles will happen. Holy thoughts and ideas will appear. Ordinary living will become precious.

Reach out to me. Ask and it shall be given. Seek and be amazed at what you find. Stand amazed in my presence. I am faithful. I promise. Rejoice!

Exodus 3:5; Deuteronomy 4:29

29

Though life seems to come at you aggressively—full force—my peace and calm can overcome it. If you will embrace me each day, you will be able to triumphantly overcome the storms of life.

Droughts of the spirit and of resources will be overcome and sated with fresh rains of my spirit. My spirit works both in the spiritual and the physical realms. If it were not so, what would be the point of your prayers?

So pray and believe—in spite of what life brings and because of what life brings. Hold your face upward and let my refreshing rains gently and thoroughly cleanse and renew. Pray and believe and be thankful. I am a constant that never changes. I am. I supply. I comfort. I guide. I love. I promise. Rejoice!

Isaiah 7:4a; Isaiah 43:10-11; Matthew 21:22

30

Allow me to sort out your confusion of thoughts, my child. Allow me to calm your spirit. You tend to begin your day with an intimidating "to-do" list before you have laid out your plans to me. Allow my spirit to work before you allow yourself to become frenzied and stressed. I bring calm. I bring peace. I bring order.

Stop your ceaseless activity and listen for my voice. You cannot hear me over the roar of your voracious activity. You fail to be still before me. Yes, you give me "lip service," taking time to absorb a devotional reading and to pray. But I want more of you than that. I want your mind, your thoughts and your spirit at rest so that I can speak to you—so that my guidance can lead you through this day. Wait for me. Quiet your thoughts. Set aside your agenda. Ask me to sit with you. I am waiting for you. I promise. Rejoice!

Exodus 14:14; Psalm 37:7a

31

In the stillness of the morning, you can find me. In the heat of the day, I am here. In the darkness of the evening, I am still with you. I will never leave you or forsake you. My promise to you—ever present, ever ready, always loving. I am your father. I am your God. Dwell on these thoughts and be thankful. Rejoice. Always rejoice!

Deuteronomy 31:8

Life Guide

AUGUST

1

Throughout your life there will be many kinds of breezes, from strong, damaging winds to soft evening whispers. If you will trust me in all things, you will weather the storms and flourish. I am the one who will guide and protect. I am the one who will see you through the storms and the night. I am the one who will love you and walk with you all your days. I am the one. Trust me. Put aside fear and worry. Count on my love for you and my presence with you.

Count on me as the only unchanging thing in your life. Count on me. Trust me. Love me. Spend time with me. Contemplate my goodness. Pray to me. I listen. I hear. I answer. I love *you*. I promise. Rejoice!

Matthew 7:24-25; II Corinthians 3:18

2

"My grace is enough; it's all you need. My strength comes into its own in your weakness." (Second Corinthians 12:8-9, *The Message*)

Sit with me, child. Just rest in my presence. Life can be overwhelming for my children at times. These times somehow make it easier for you to turn to me. I am always present, but in these times of great need, you turn and desperately seek my face. So this morning, I turn my face to you. My light shines on you, my comfort surrounds you, my healing works within you, my love encompasses you, and you realize that I am with you. Always. I promise. Rejoice!

3

It is good to sometimes contemplate the past. Good when you can draw from positive memories and from your thoughts of how I have been faithful to see you through difficult situations and trying times. Always remember to follow these travels into your past with gratitude to me, your Heavenly Father. Think on the things that are true and pure and encouraging. Try to contemplate how good has come to your life, and be thankful.

I am a God of promise and possibility. I am your father, who desires good for you in the now and in the then—past, present and future. I promise. Rejoice!

Deuteronomy 7:9; I Corinthians 1:9

4

"…Don't you see, you planned evil against me, but God used those same plans for my good…" (Genesis 50:19-21)

And so it is with you, my children. What another may have planned in evil (selfishness, ego), I will turn to good. For I know the plans I have for you—plans for good and not for evil. Do not allow others to cloud my vision for you. Do not allow bitterness to taint your thoughts. Follow the lead of Joseph and shower love even on those who are your enemies. Love wins every time. Love others, and trust in me.

I have plans for you that will lift your spirits. Love abundantly. Sow love as seeds wherever you are able. The harvest of love will return to you, and you will be thankful. I promise. Rejoice!

Jeremiah 29:11

5

When it seems as if all is crashing down around you; when discouragement fills your very soul; when you feel paralyzed by the world and the circumstances in which you live—turn. Turn to me. I am your father.

When you can turn from all the things of life that cause you anxiety and stress and look full into the light of my presence, all the worries and woes of life fade into shadows, and your soul lifts at the radiance before you. It is difficult for my children to turn away from the concerns of life, but do not despair. For I am always with you. I bring you help and comfort. Through me, you receive the heavenly power to turn and rejoice in me. I am able to do all things—to guide, to lead, to hold you close. I am able. I promise. So rejoice, my children. Rejoice!

Joshua 1:9

6

You may feel sometimes that time is passing quickly, child, but I am a timeless God. I am the God of always—yesterday, today, tomorrow. Always with you. Always providing. Always protecting. Always loving. Always.

Time does not constrain me. Time is not my enemy, and neither is it yours. So go forth focusing not on time, but on me. I am blessing your moments and your days until time will be no more for you—until you will be with me and your loved ones for eternity. I promise. Rejoice!

Ecclesiastes 3:11-15

7

Draw nigh to me, child. Just rest in my presence. Let go of fears and worries and wounds. Let go of preconceived ideas about situations and about others. Look at all with fresh eyes. Cover your lenses with love and compassion and kindness. Walk in my light.

Practice each day, and you will find your heart and your steps are lighter. Do as I lead you to do. Say what I nudge you to say. Blessings will follow. I promise. Rejoice!

Psalm 89:15

8

"Get rid of all bitterness, rage and anger, brawling and slander, along with every form of malice. Be kind and compassionate to one another, forgiving each other, just as in Christ God forgave you." (Ephesians 4:31-32)

Order. I created order in the universe, and when things in your life are orderly, you are more apt to find peace.

Day, night, seasons, solstices, years...I created them all. Follow me, and there will be order in your spiritual lives. Follow me, and you will find joy and peace.

Do not allow the *dis*-order of the world to distract you from my presence or my plan for you. Turn from disorder and focus on me.

I promise you love and peace and joy. Rejoice!

9

Enough. I provide for you, and what you receive is "enough." Enough for the moment. Enough for the day. Enough for the situation.

Do not confuse "enough" with "plenty." Plenty is more *your* word than mine.

I specialize in moments, and in those moments I am with you, giving you just what you need.

Your idea of need satisfaction and mine are not always the same. I satisfy your needs. I give you enough love and compassion and courage and energy for whatever comes your way. I give you these tools so that you can be my feet and hands and voice and heart for others. I bless you in this way always. I give you enough. I promise. Rejoice!

John 6:31-35

10

Cleanse me, and I shall be whiter than snow.

When you think of cleansing, you think of soap and water. But my cleansing comes from the spirit—the light of my presence. For in this light all things are made known and you see yourself clearly, as I have always seen.

So pray for cleansing—for purity—and pray for grace. By so doing, my child, you will align yourself even more closely with me. Seek me, and you will find blessings beyond measure. I promise. Rejoice!

Psalm 51:7; Hebrews 10:22-25

11

Go forth with confidence that I can and will look after my children. Seek to do my will in all things. Ask me for guidance, for words and even for thoughts. Let me saturate and permeate your very being. Seek in all things to follow me, and I will be faithful to answer each request. I promise. Rejoice!

Luke 11:9-10

12

The ravages that life on earth extracts, the difficulties that fill your days, the disappointments and hurts—these are a part of living the human life.

This is why I encourage my children to turn to me—to sit at my feet.

Should you choose to concentrate on these problems, you will lose the joy of believing and trusting in me. You will lose the opportunity I am giving you to praise me, to thank me, to show others your faith in the midst of it all.

So turn. Pray. Sit patiently at my feet and share my love with others. Push joy to the forefront and shine for me in this broken world. You will find blessing if you do. I promise. Rejoice!

II Chronicles 6:38-39; Acts 3:19-20

13

Be still. Know that I am God. In all you do this day, be still. Wait before you resume furious activity. Wait to see how I lead you. Wait before you speak. Wait to see how I guide you.

Though you think you are doing my will by serving me, you often jump out ahead of my will with your words and deeds. Be still and wait. And when you can do this, your life, your actions and your words will be a blessing for yourself and for others. I promise. Rejoice!

Psalm 46:10-11; Romans 8:25-26

14

Love and obey. Tune in to my wishes and desires for your life.

This life is not an idle exercise. It is, in fact, an opportunity for you to choose me. An opportunity, given to you over and over, to choose love. An opportunity to turn to me for everything:

—When you are anxious
—When you are joyful
—When you have negative thoughts
—When you think and when you speak and when you pray
—When things are not to your liking, and when things are going well.

Give me every circumstance of your life. This does not come easily to my children, but this coming to me, this *choosing* my way and choosing me, allows me to work more fully and completely in your lives.

If you cannot choose me, how can I speak to you? How can I inhabit your heart? I desire your companionship. I desire your trust, and I desire a relationship with you. The gift of your love and your choices (to pray; to come unto me) are priceless to me. I will reward you for those choices with a peace and a joy that surpass explanation. I promise. Rejoice!

Jeremiah 7:23; Psalm 5:11

15

The beasts of the field and the birds of the air—all part of God's glorious world. How great thou art!

I am a God who is concerned with the little things—the details of this universe. I am a God who loves completely, fully and unconditionally.

My children consider themselves most important in my eyes, but that is not so. All of creation is important—essential—to me. I love with a love that cannot be comprehended. I love with abandon. My children cannot fathom the height and width and depth of my love for them. But it is there, and it is eternal. I promise. Rejoice!

Genesis 1:20-22; Romans 8:38-39

16

For safety
For love and kindness
For wisdom and discernment
For openness to you
Father, I pray.

You are under the shadow of my wings. Be faithful to turn to me. Be diligent to pray for those who come your way. Be attuned to my spirit within you. Life is not easy, but life with me is a deeper life. Move and listen and wait and think, and let these things be done with the knowledge that I am with you. I am beside you and within you. I never leave you. I am joyful when you recognize my presence, but I am here even when you do not. Rest in the comfort and knowledge that your *father* loves you. I promise. Rejoice!

Psalm 57:1; Psalm 63:7-8

17

Remember to thank me. Give me your praise in all things, even when you think life is difficult, and even when circumstances do not turn out as you would like. At all times and in all things, give me your thanks.

Your mind will be changed, your heart will soften, your spirit will rejoice when you choose to be thankful.

So much of life is up to you and the choices you make. Will you choose fear or trust? Will you choose sadness or joy? Will you choose anger or satisfaction? Will you choose yourself or me?

Choose ye this day whom ye will serve. I will give you freedom to choose. Will you choose me? I have chosen you. I promise. Rejoice!

Joshua 24:15

18

I am thankful, Lord,
—for this time
—for this place
—for my family
—for my friends
—for what lies ahead, and for what has transpired to bring me to this moment, this quiet moment.

Cherish times with me, child. Cherish times when you "hear" my voice and when pen goes to paper to write down these thoughts. Be thankful in these times.

I am more than thankful, Lord. I am amazed in your presence.

There are times ahead that will call for you to trust me more. Do not worry. Do not allow fear to dominate your life. Do not succumb to the ways of the world. Depend on me. Look to me for comfort and help. I will never, ever leave you. I am always here. Take time to call out to me. Take time to listen for my voice—my words for you—and I will answer.

When you seek me, you will find me. You will weather the storms of life with victory. Your light will shine for others because it will be my light that they see. I am your father and your friend. I will never forsake you. Trust me. I will bring you through anything that challenges you. I promise. Rejoice!

Jeremiah 39:18

19

You are needed for my work in this place—this part of my world. Stay close to me, and I will send you your instructions each day. You will hear these "instructions" in different ways—thoughts, voices, communications—and you will not always recognize that these needs, these directions, are from me. But stay very close to me, and in so doing, you can be assured of following my desires for your actions—for your life.

Live normally. Love as I love, without placing your own conditions on life. Be joy-filled, and I will insure that joy continues to flow. Be careful to listen for my still small nudgings—my voice. And in return, I will answer you, and I will bless you beyond measure. Tears will fill you and overflow at the goodness that will come your way. I promise. Rejoice!

Psalm 126:3

20

For the ability to experience tiny miracles, I thank you, Lord.

Cherish each moment you have. Do not be anxious for what lies ahead, either in anticipation or in worry. Instead, relish the miracle of the moment:

- the beauty of the sunrise
- the songs of the birds
- the flowers and their intricate construction
- the many colors of a sunset
- the refreshment of a shower

Relish the moments and be thankful.

This earth was not created to bring you problems but to bring you joy. Stand amazed! My presence is everywhere you look. My love encompasses all. So stop the fretting! Stop the worry! Stop fearing the future! Rest in me, and allow the blessings I have put into place to wash over you. You will be changed forever when you do. I promise. Rejoice!

Philippians 4:6-7

21

There will be showers of blessing for you and for those whom you love and for those for whom you pray. These showers are coming even though you feel that you see no evidence of them. My blessings do not always take the form that you expect, but they are my blessings, nonetheless.

Do you trust me? Even in this environment of uncertainty? Are you allowing worry and fear to creep into your life, your thoughts? Banish those imposters now! Turn to me. Talk to me. Trust in me. I am here—at hand—ready to listen to your heart, to walk alongside you. Ready, always ready, to answer your prayers and to bring peace and joy into your life. Trust me. I am worthy of your trust. I promise. Rejoice!

Ezekiel 34:26; Psalm 25:2-5

22

Do you give Christianity a bad name? When others see you, do they see that joy? That peace? That love and compassion in you? Or do you wear a cloak of darkness? Are you sour? Are you angry? Are you negative? Are you depressed? Are you disappointed in this life?

My children, it is my wish for you that others would want to come to me because they sense my presence in your life. You do me a *dis*-service when you allow the burdens of life to wear you down. Do you think you are the *only* one in this world who suffers? You are not. Life brings with it many facets—like the facets of a prism. So *shine!* Let my light shine through your eyes and your attitude. Expect good and expect joy. Pour yourself out for others. Remove the focus from yourself. Love me. Cherish me, and be glad. Allow your glad heart to be infectious, just like a joyful virus. Go forth and spread the germs of joy. Watch the germination of joy in others. You will be the one who is blessed. I promise. Rejoice!

Numbers 6:25-26; Isaiah 60:1; II Corinthians 4:6; Philippians 2:14-16

23

For quiet moments
—for abundant life
—for new friends and old
—for new experiences and for memories

Lord, I thank thee.

I have been faithful to you each and every day to more than meet your needs. I have brought you opportunities for growth and chances for adventures you never thought possible. I care about your every thought, need and action. You are my beloved child. I created my children, and it brings me joy to shower you all with love and surprise.

Anticipate miracles. Look for the work of my hand. Life is not built on coincidences but on my plans and on my miracles, moment by moment and day by day.

Stop your busy life long enough to recognize the works of my hands. Stop to appreciate what I place in your path. Anticipate what I may have for you in your future.

I am a faithful and loving God. I promise. Rejoice!

Deuteronomy 7:9; Psalm 31:5; I Corinthians 1:9

24

Think on these things:
> All that is true
> All that is love
> All that is eternal
> All that is pure
> All that is nurturing
> All that is positive
> All that is unselfish
> All that brings trust
> All that brings peace
> All that brings joy.

And I will help you and encourage you and eternally walk with you. I promise. Rejoice!

Philippians 4:8-9

25

Keep me, Jesus, in the shadow of your wings.

These truly are trying times for my children, times that you cannot understand. But you do not need to understand the times. You need, instead, to draw close to me. Allow me to work in your life and in your circumstances. How else can you appreciate the miracle of my presence? If all in life were easy, if all life's troubles were easily solved, what would draw you to me?

Consider this: I am here. I am listening. I am love. What more do you need?

Turn to me with your joys and with your sorrows. Turn to me with your successes and with your challenges. I am waiting, willing to help you. I am anxious to walk and talk with you. What are you waiting for? Trust not on your own understanding. Trust not on the things of this world. Those things are not sure. They are not real. Instead, turn to me for all your hopes and dreams. Turn to me to walk you through the rough times. Turn to me, and I will love and guide you. You will be amazed. I promise. Rejoice!

Psalm 17:8

26

You know my heart and you know my prayers even before I utter them, Father. Listen to my mind and my heart. Work in the lives of those whom you bring to my mind. You know the paths you have for each of them. I want your very best for each of them. You are my rock and my fortress. I depend on you and on your goodness.

I do know your heart. I know your thoughts. I know that you want to be connected to my spirit at all times. And yet, I also know your weaknesses and your sorrow when you perceive that you have failed me. Do not fret. I have not left you. I will not leave you. That is my promise. I will love you forever. You are my precious child. I have formed you as if you were the very first person. I am a loving, tending God and Father. I promise. Rejoice!

I Chronicles 29:17a; Deuteronomy 31:8

27

Do you have faith? Are you believing in me? Do you believe in miracles? Do you trust me with the cares, worries and concerns of life? Stop and ask yourself right this moment: What is stronger, God or the world in which you live? Pray for my will to be done. Pray for my guidance and direction. Wait on me. Lift your concerns, but as you pray, child, *believe*. Believe in the God of the universe. Believe in my holy spirit, and believe in my son.

All things are possible to those who believe in me and trust me. Ask, and I will answer. Seek me, and I will be found by you. Knock on my door, and I will answer. Believe, and I will be faithful. I promise. Rejoice!

I John 5:13-15

28

Your family, your friends, yourself—all are safely in my care. You all have lessons to learn. You all fall short of what is my best for you. You all need to rely on me and me alone.

Lean not on your own understanding. (That is in my word.) But trust me, talk with me, lean on me. I want good for you. I am trustworthy. You know these truths. Now live my truth. Love those who cross your path. Love even those who do not seem worthy or who are un-lovely. Love with abandon. Love completely. Love unconditionally. Love extravagantly. I do. I promise. Rejoice!

Psalm 59:17; Proverbs 3:5-6

29

For the peace of this home,
for the love in this home,
for the people in this place,
I pray and
I give you thanks.

Peace and prosperity are yours. Claim them now. I do not give gifts lightly, nor do I give gifts that the world understands. It is so with these gifts. Peace in the midst of life's storm, and riches of my kingdom. Reach out and grasp these gifts. They are for you—for this moment.

I know the plans I have for you. Believe in me, and believe in my faithfulness. I am your loving father. I promise. Rejoice!

John 14:27; Jeremiah 29:11

30

Be thankful. Express your gratitude. Do not wait for the "big" things, but remember to be thankful for all the little things in life. Spend time each day thinking of all those incidentals that you might normally overlook, and express your gratitude for each one.

Is it a brush with nature? An observation? Stand amazed and grateful for my creation. Is it a meal when you hunger or a roof of protection from the rain? Be thankful for my provisions. In *all* things give thanks, and you will reap the blessings of my kingdom. I promise. Rejoice!

Psalm 147:7; I Chronicles 16:34; Revelation 11:17

31

Blessed assurance, Jesus is mine. Oh what a foretaste of glory divine.[12]

And so shall it be—when hearts are united with me, glory awaits. You have that assurance. Invest your time with me now, and there are surely glorious blessings awaiting you in the future. Much like monetary investments on earth, you invest your treasures in hopes of gaining more riches. Concentrate instead on investing your personal resources—time, heart, attention, prayers, thoughts—in me, and the spiritual riches that will follow will not be able to be contained. I am a God of abundance, and I long to shower you with blessings beyond earthly measure. I promise. Rejoice!

Hebrews 10:22-23

Life Guide

SEPTEMBER

1

"Help me, Holy Spirit." In all things, in all ways, I need your help.

Father, Son and Holy Spirit are waiting and listening and hearing your prayers. The Three-in-One hears both spoken and unspoken cries of the heart. Blessings will shower down. Tears will be dried. Joyful hearts and peaceful spirits will result because my children pray.

There is no circumstance too difficult for me. There is no situation I cannot handle. I stand at the door and wait for my children to come to me. Seek my presence. Long for my face. Pray, pray, pray, and you will find comfort and solace. You will know me in a deeper sense, and our bonds of communication will grow stronger. Our love will grow, and you will glow with the joy of the Holy Spirit. Seek me and you will find me. I promise. Rejoice!

Matthew 28:19-20

2

My wonders will never cease. Stand amazed in my presence. Prepare your hearts to accept the gifts of love and guidance I will send your way. It is my intention to do good in your lives. It is my desire that you recognize my handiwork when good comes your way. Ask, and you shall receive. Pray, and then patiently wait for my answers.

I will bless you, and you will become a blessing for others when you share words of my wondrous works in your life. This is the flow of life—the flow of spirit. When you fail to share the stories of my working, you stop the flow of my blessings.

My word is just that—the sharing of stories of how I have worked in this world. Those stories allow my blessings to continue to flow. So share! Go tell my people what you know of me. In so doing, blessings will flow *from* you and *to* you. I promise. Rejoice!

Psalm 16:11; Genesis 49:25-26a

3

There are seasons in nature and seasons in life. My children experience these seasons of youth and age, joy and sorrow. Be of good cheer, because I am with you always.

I am a part of the lowest lows, the highest highs, and all the times in between. I love and cherish my creations. I want you to acknowledge my presence and to rest in it. Grasp the peace and joys that are sent your way. Hold on to them as a light, and let that light of remembrance serve to illuminate your lives when difficulties arise.

Do not delude yourselves. You will face difficult times. But always, always, turn to me. Always remember my faithfulness to you. Be certain of my presence. Trust and believe, because I am a faithful father and God. I promise. Rejoice!

Psalm 104:19; II Corinthians 12:10

4

Fear not, for I am with you. Though you see me not, I am present. Though life brings feelings of helplessness and hopelessness, those feelings are imposters. I am a God of hope and help. I am love and promise.

Believe on me. Trust in me. Place your times in my hands. I am always at work. The world as you know it is also an imposter. Real truth and reality are with me. Trust. Be faithful to believe in me. I am here. I promise. Rejoice!

Psalm 146:5; John 14:11-14

5

Do not despair, for I am the one who hears your prayers and who answers. You grow impatient. Your need to control drives you to believe that your prayers are *not* answered. But my child, I am God. I always hear. I always answer. It is left to you to obey, to believe and to trust. There is nothing too small for me and nothing too large. I am a compassionate and caring God. Ask, and you shall receive. I promise. Rejoice!

II Corinthians 4:8-9; Daniel 9:17-18

6

Walk in the way I have prepared for you. Take care as you walk that you stay close to me, your Father and your God. I am holding your hand. I am watching for stumbling blocks. I am ensuring that your journey is safe.

Do not try to run ahead of me. Do not fearfully lag behind me. Walk with me. Walk confidently. Walk. Walk. Walk.

Walk when you'd rather rest. Walk when you'd prefer to run. Stay close to me. Savor my presence. And when you do, you will be blessed by the fellowship we share. You will be enlightened by my teachings in your life. You will find comfort in my protection, and you will find peace in my presence. An overwhelming sense of joy will wash over you, and you will walk on, secure and safe.

Do not allow the world to plant distrust in the garden of your heart. Do not entertain thoughts of failure or disappointment. Instead, look up into the sunshine of my countenance and trust me to guide your path.

You will find blessing in the pathways I choose. You will find contentment for your soul. You will find understanding, and you will have an overwhelming desire to share these truths with others. I am an ever-present help for you as you live this earthly life. I promise. Rejoice!

Deuteronomy 5:32-33; Psalm 15:2-5; Job 36:11; I Timothy 6:6

7

Sounds of nature, sounds of this world—all can serve to draw your thoughts and mind away from me. Sit quietly before me. Release your thoughts to me, even as they begin to form in your mind. And wait for me to speak to you. I speak in many ways. If only you can be attuned to me, you can "hear" me.

This day spreads out before you. Listen. Hear. Be encouraged. Shower love through your thoughts and through your presence. My love will flow through you to ease another's earthly load. This I promise. So be open to me. Today. Do not let the world overcome you, for I have overcome the world. I promise. Rejoice!

I John 5:4-5

8

Come to me, those who feel weak and heavy-laden, and I will give you rest. Rest for your weary soul. Do not grow weary from well-doing, my child. I am here to guide and assist—to direct your ways.

The weary spirit is often a result of you moving ahead of me, intent on your own agenda. You set your mind on your own goals and then wonder why I, your father, allow the weariness to descend on you.

The lesson is this: Set your eyes on *me*. I will carry you to the goals I have for you. While you may tire in the process, you will not grow weary. There *is* a difference.

My children always fall back to worldly ways and worldly goals. I am not of this world. My goals and desires for you are different. Decide today to follow my ways. Decide over and over to follow me. And in so doing, you will find glorious peace and rest. I promise. Rejoice!

Matthew 11:28

9

You know and you have been reminded that Jesus, my son, loved and gave of himself only to discover that he was disdained and even crucified by those he sought to embrace. Why would you think your own life will be different?

You are seeking love, encouragement, acceptance, acknowledgment from flawed creatures of this earth. No person can humanly meet your needs. Only your Father in Heaven can give you what you need. When will you learn this lesson? When will you cast your eyes to me for the things that really matter? When will you cease trying to have all your needs met by those who are incapable of so doing?

You have many lessons to learn. Can you begin today to release your need to control? Practice! Practice placing those hurts at my feet. Practice choosing love, even in the face of disdain. Practice!

I am always here. It is my deepest desire to help you. I love you, my child, with a love and an acceptance that surpass all you can imagine. I promise. Rejoice!

Leviticus 19:18; Proverbs 3:3-6

10

Lift your thoughts and feelings out of the muddy mire, child. Leave them behind. Turn your eyes toward me. There is no stain where I am. Feelings evaporate in my presence. Only truth reigns. And the essential truth? Love. So practice loving others.

Think of others. Who among your friends and family needs my love and help? Who is hurting? Who is struggling? Who deals with situations much worse than yours? There are too many to count. Grab my hand and let me lead you in paths that are cobbled in love.

Love without counting the cost. Love with abandon. Love without expecting anything in return. Love my people and my creatures. Love, love, love. And when you do as I ask, you will be amazed at how your hurts and fears and worries are diminished.

Cast your eyes to me and away from yourself. The world of hope and possibility will open up for you. A world filled with love. I promise. Rejoice!

John 13:34-35

11

Change. My children often become anxious in the face of change. But I tell you, child, that change is inherent in life. If you live, you change. Change is an absolute.

The changes that take place around you are miraculous. If only you could see change as a blessing—my blessing—for you. It is for your ultimate good. A seed changes to become a plant that produces food to nourish you. A sunrise becomes a sunset which becomes a sunrise again. Never the same, always changing. Change is a constant of life.

Let go of your fears of the unknown, of change, and embrace the miraculous possibilities the future can bring to you. Put aside dread and wrap yourself in hope and anticipation. You will be surprised by joy! I promise. Rejoice!

James 1:17; Isaiah 44:3

12

Fear. Do not let a spirit of fear paralyze you, child.

This fear is behind all your concerns. You fear what lies ahead. You fear, and your fear indicates a lack of trust in me.

I am your rock. I am your fortress. I am your future. I am your father. I am your God.

Turn from fear into a pathway to freedom. Turn to a life filled with my spirit. I will secure your future. I already have. You must believe. I am faithful. I promise! Rejoice!

Psalm 18:2; Hebrews 13:6

13

Provider. Protector. Father. Ruler. Creator. These are only a few of the words you need to grasp as you ponder your Father in Heaven.

You create your own troubles when you worry and fret. That sort of life is not what I have in mind for you.

When you live in the present moment, there is gratitude and peace. When you do not allow your mind to leap ahead into the unknown, there is serenity. It is so hard for you to refrain from leaping ahead of me.

Just for this moment, this hour, this day, seek to enjoy your moments. Be grateful for how I have protected you (during the storms). Be thankful for all that I have made available for you. Find joy in my love for you. And be at peace.

It truly is possible. I promise. Rejoice!

Leviticus 26:6a; Colossians 3:15-17

14

Rest. I bring rest to my weary children. When life seems to overcome you, come to me. In me you will find rest and peace.

I am concerned for your well-being. I love you and desire the best for you. You often get distracted by the ebbs and flows of life. The circumstances that surround you cause anxiety and stress in your life. So come to me, you who are weary and heavy-laden, and I will bring you peace and rest. I promise. Rejoice!

Psalm 16:9, 11; Psalm 62:5-8; Acts 2:26-28

15

You stand at the door and knock, yet you think I do not hear your cries and pleas. You are convinced that I am not listening, that I have turned from you.

You must trust me. You must believe that I hear and that I answer. These times of trial for you are necessary so that you can fully understand that I do hear. I do listen. I do answer.

But there is more at stake here than your pleas for a quick answer to your prayers. Your future is awaiting. There are great and new things ahead for you. Do not take this time lightly. Believe in me—that I can do all things. Trust me—that I am going ahead of you to prepare the way.

Just as a farmer plows up an overgrown field, you will soon be plowing new ground. As you work this new field for me, abundance will shower you in new ways. Get ready, children. I have plans for your future. I promise. Rejoice!

Revelation 3:20; I John 3:23-24

16

A place of peace awaits you. Reach out your hands and claim my peace. It does not exist in the world. It exists within your spirit, so claim your peace.

I am the great provider, and I give you all the things that you need— peace, joy, love, compassion. These are things not easily attained in the world (the physical world), but the abundance of these things awaits your taking in the spiritual world.

So reach out your hands and your heart and accept my gift of peace to you. It is a precious gift to you and to all my children who wait upon me. I promise. Rejoice!

I Peter 1:8-9; II Peter 1:2

17

While your life may be going well, the lives of others may be in turmoil. It is much like hurricane season. Where the path of the hurricane is moving, there is fear, anxiety, destruction. And just out of the range of the storm, there is sunshine and peace.

So it is with life. Much is going on with each life I love. Never forget the truth that I am always loving you, child. Whether you are in the midst of a storm or basking in the sunlight of my presence, I am love.

In the good times, praise me. In the good times, remember to pray for those who are in the midst of a storm—those whose hearts are sad or anxious or fearful.

When you are experiencing darkness, there are others of my children who will be petitioning me on your behalf.

That is how this world is meant to work. I am lord of all, and I touch my children's heart to care for their sisters and brothers. So when a person—a child of mine—comes to mind, lift them to me in prayer. They may have needs and hurts that you know not of. They may be deep in the darkness of life, and your prayer on their behalf may make a difference in their day—in their life. In just this way will I tap others to pray for you.

Such is the way of a life with me. It is a life of love and compassion and encouragement. It is a life of purpose. It is a life that makes a difference. It is a life that prepares you for an eternity with me. I promise. Rejoice!

Luke 8:24-25; James 5:13-16

18

Do you doubt my presence with you? Whenever you doubt, look around you. Listen. Watch. I am here, ever present.

From devotions you read (and that amaze you at how relevant they are to your life), to people who love you, to nature that surrounds you—*I am* speaking. *I am* here with you.

Do not doubt. Only believe. Be sure that I am God, and I am always with you.

Be watchful in the days ahead for all the many ways I am working to ensure blessings in your life. For the ways I am guiding your future. For the directions I am sending your way. For your safety and health and bountiful future. I am here. I will not be waylaid, nor will I be stopped in my efforts to pour my love into your life. I promise. Rejoice!

Matthew 21:21-22

19

Plant seeds and watch them grow. This will give you insight into the world of my spirit. When you truly contemplate growth and maturation and regeneration from a seed, you catch a glimpse of the great things I can do with and in the lives of my children.

Just as there are many varieties of seeds—looking not only so different from each other, but also resembling nothing like the mature plant—so are my children and the possibilities within each of you different.

Look at the clues to understanding me that I have placed before you. Ask me to help you understand on a spiritual level, not just on an intellectual level, and I will open your spirit to vistas of understanding. Your faith will deepen. Your life will be richer. I promise. Rejoice!

Mark 4:30-32

20

Busy! You are surrounded by a busy world, and you so easily get caught up in it all. You "buy into" the world's view that you must not "waste" your time, that you must always be productive. You need something to show for each day as it comes to an end. You need concrete justification that your days and your years leave something to show others.

What if I told you, child, that what you need to do is spend your time on something the world cannot evaluate?

What if I told you that what is truly lasting and meaningful is something that cannot be seen or touched?

Practice my presence. Seek my will. Let go of the expectations of the world you inhabit.

Love. Pray. Spread joy and compassion. Intercede for others. Seek my will. Be a living testament to me. Rely on my spirit. You will be amazed at the results. I promise. Rejoice!

Deuteronomy 4:29-31; Hebrews 7:25

21

Pray and praise. Pray and praise. As you walk through this day, pray and praise, for both are important and need to be done together.

Think of children who only express their wants and needs, expecting all their demands and wishes to be met. So it is with me when my children only demand and petition. When these prayers are coupled with praise, there is joy for me *and* for you. Because when praises (thanks) are offered, there is a warm joy and pleasure that unfolds. I promise. Rejoice!

Exodus 15:2; James 5:13

22

My storehouse is filled for you, but the workers will reap far more from it than those who are miserly with the time they spend with me. I have told you to pray as you go, to spend time with me, to worship me and to love me. When you do these things that I ask of you, then the blessings of my storehouse will fill the bucket of your soul and your life.

Do not misunderstand—I *will* answer the prayers of my children. But the answers will fall bounteously for those who have learned to pray and to listen for my voice.

With this time and learning, my children know that I *do* answer, but not always as they should prescribe or demand. No! I answer in my own wisdom and grace, according to my desire to work out my plan in your life for this life, and for the next.

Once again—time spent with me fleshes out in love, compassion, grace, truth. Whatever comes, my children can be confident that I am with them. I promise. Rejoice!

Deuteronomy 28:12; Malachi 3:10-12

23

The ability to trust me is a gift given to all my children. Whatever makes you anxious, whatever makes you worry, whatever brings you fear, I have already countered by promising you that you can choose to trust me for it all.

So very often you try to trust, but around the edges of your efforts creep fringes of worry and anxiety and fear. Whenever that occurs, cease all your doing and ask me to carry those burdens. Trust me to answer those prayers. Rest confidently that *I am* working in the situation that causes you to fret. I am always working on your behalf. I am always wanting to bring good to you. I am able to find solutions to your every problem, your every concern. So trust me.

I have proven myself faithful in the past. Prove yourself faithful now. Trust and be patient as solutions come your way, as answers appear. Once again, I tell you I am faithful to answer when you call. I promise. Rejoice!

Psalm 22:9; Jeremiah 39:18; Hebrews 2:13

24

This is the day that the Lord has made. Let us rejoice and be glad in it.

Rejoice. Praise me. Look and listen for me in all that surrounds you—the people whom you meet, the animals and all of nature. Listen and hear the sounds of rejoicing.

Pray for those who cross your path. Send love to all—not only those you see with your eyes, but those who are in your heart.

Pray. Praise. Rejoice. In this way, you are following the path I have laid before you. I promise. And again I say: Rejoice!

Deuteronomy 4:39; Psalm 118:24

25

You need to be consistent in turning to me, children. Do not just go through your daily "motions," even though these motions may be good things. Take time to be quiet before me, and listen. Listen in that quiet for my still, small voice. I have things to say to you. I have guidance to offer you. I have love to share with you. I have comfort to spread over you. I have guidance to give you and encouragement for your days. So listen. Hear. Heed. Blessings will abound. I promise. Rejoice!

Isaiah 32:17-18; Psalm 71:21

26

Peace. Relax your anxious muscles. Release your overactive thoughts. Rest in my presence. If only for a while, cast your list of chores away and wait for my direction and leading, for this is the day the Lord has made. Rejoice and be glad in it.

If you will begin each day with me, you will soon feel my joy with you as you go. I promise. Again I say: Rejoice!

I Chronicles 16:10-11; I John 1:4

27

Give me the mind of God, insomuch as I am able to accept it. Make my thoughts eternal—not of this world. Place the prayers you desire in my heart, Lord.

The world in which you live and move has chosen to focus on negative thoughts, on "woe-is-me" philosophy. And when you focus on the ever-streaming "news," how can your minds even comprehend that this news is not real? In the way of the world, it is very real. Loss of ethics, loss of character, financial worries, egocentric thinking, terror, loss of morality—the list goes on.

But it remains for my children to understand that their reality is not of this world. The reality for my followers is spirit. You cannot touch the spirit with your physical being, only with your spirit. The spirit is positive. The spirit is redeeming. The spirit is a teacher. The spirit is forgiving. The spirit is love. The spirit is the Trinity—Father, Son and Spirit. When you dwell in the spirit, you dwell with me. I promise. Rejoice!

Colossians 3:12-17; Psalm 51:11-12

28

I am a God of the delightful and of the unexpected. I am creator and designer of the universe. I am power and humility…and all that is in between. But most of all, I am love.

My children lack understanding of who and what I am. They labor and struggle through their lives and make those lives so difficult. If only each of you could realize how closeness to me can make lives different.

The messages of my word are misunderstood. The times for closeness and fellowship with me are few. The living out of my truth and love by my children in this world is even less evident.

Follow me. Allow yourselves to spend time with me. Let me fill your lives with my spirit. When this happens in your life, you too will have experiences that are delightful and unexpected. I promise. Rejoice!

Isaiah 40:28; Exodus 31:3; I Kings 4:29; Proverbs 2:6

29

Shout for joy, all the earth. Morning has broken. A new day has arrived, and with it comes a clean slate. Relish each moment. Do not succumb to fretting or worry, either about the past or about the future. The past is behind you. You can change no part of it. The future is ahead of you, and unknown. Worry and anxious thoughts change nothing. So enjoy this moment by observing, praying, communing, living and loving, for that is what I created you to do. Be about your father's business, and when you choose this path, peace will enfold you. I promise. Rejoice!

Psalm 35:27-28

30

Be still and know that I am God. (Psalm 46:10a)

(I am still, Lord. And I know you.)

And I know you, my child, because I made you, and you have chosen to be mine. I have made all of creation and have chosen all people, but your gift to me, your Heavenly Father, is when you choose me. The longing I have is for my children to turn from the false glitter of the world and embrace the true riches of a relationship with me, and to come and dwell in my kingdom.

I shout for joy when my children come home. Coming home does not necessarily mean a departure from earth in a physical way (death). It means that my children choose to turn to me (death to sin). Each chooses to walk with me, talk with me, and listen to me speak to their hearts. Oh, how I desire that two-way conversation. Oh, how the blessings flow.

Be still before me. I will come. I promise. Rejoice!

Psalm 139:13

Life Guide
OCTOBER

1

All is well. Though seemingly all around you is failing, just remember, my children: All is well. Through your worries, through your fears, you can change nothing but to turn to me. So turn. When this world seems a hopeless place, turn to me. When all you have depended on fails, turn to me. I am the solid rock on which your life is built. I hear your groans and know your worries. I also know your heart and your desires. So trust me. Trust me in the good times and in the trying times. Keep the light of hope alive in your lives so *you* can be a beacon of hope to others. Let others see my light shining through you.

II Samuel 22:29-37; Isaiah 57:10; Ephesians 1:18-21

2

The only constant in the physical world is change. But just as the ocean tides come and go—just as the seasons repeat their cycles—the *constant* of change brings comfort. Settle in front of nature and watch my work. Know. Believe. Trust. Love. Pray. This is the truth. I promise. Rejoice!

James 1:17

3

Worship me in the beauty of the holiness of my creation. Worship me in hymns of praise that spring to your mind. Worship me in the unexpected. Worship me as you go, taking care to examine each circumstance, each happening, as an opportunity and even, perhaps, as a miracle I have wrought.

Worship me in the unstructured times of your life as well as in those that have been planned.

Give each moment, each hour, as your ongoing gift to me. Expect nothing in return, but be ever amazed at the blessings that will follow you.

Pray as a part of your worship. Sing. Meditate. Observe. Listen. Love. And you will see me. I promise. Rejoice!

I Chronicles 16:29b; Luke 4:8; Habakkuk 1:5; John 5:20

4

Fear not, for I have redeemed you. (Isaiah 43:1b)

Though you are surrounded by fear from unbelievers…though you are in the midst of many who cannot understand or comprehend my goodness and love…persevere. Practice forgiveness. Practice compassion. I will uphold you. I will enable you to be strong. I am truth. I am love. I promise. Rejoice!

5

Peace I give you. Peace in the midst of the storms of life. Peace in the midst of the showers of blessing. Peace in the good times and in those times you deem "difficult." Could those times be "difficult" because you lack trust in me? Do you believe I am faithful to lead you? Do you believe I can be trusted with your cares and hurts, and with your dreams? Do you not believe I am greater than life's most challenging situations?

You must examine your heart. Your problems are not with me. They are within yourselves. Trust. Obey. Believe. Have faith. Love. Put aside the dramas in life. Put aside your own selfish agendas. Allow me to work. I am faithful to accomplish miraculous things in your life and in the lives of others. I promise. Rejoice!

John 14:27

6

Oh, my child, if only you could let go of yourself and cling to me, you would be amazed at how your life on earth would flow. You are a spiritual being, but all you can see are your physical attributes.

I mean for good to flow to and through you. I intend for your earthly life to be a blessing to others. You will learn (as you go) that by being my blessing for others, you, too, will be blessed.

Accept my love and guidance as you observe nature. The birds that flock to the feeder are not worried about where their next meal will be found. Your pets trust you to love them and provide for them. If these animals can trust so freely, can it not be so with you?

Let my love and my provision for you flow—like a stream, like a river, like a wave washing over you with blessings.

Rejoice in the moments that you have. Trust me to do good. Believe that I am a faithful father. For that is the truth. I promise. Rejoice!

Psalm 9:10; Romans 5:17; Psalm 105:41-45

7

For the challenges and the struggles in life, Father, I thank you. Without them, we humans would carry on believing we are in control and that we have everything "under" control. But with them? We realize our many inadequacies and our need to depend on you. You are our awesome God.

For my children, my creation, I am thankful. I am thankful when each of you chooses to spend time with me. I am thankful when you choose to heed my will—my direction for your life, moment-by-moment. It brings *me* joy when you choose love and when you treat others with love and compassion. A life with me, following me, is not a difficult thing. It really can be quite simple. Put aside your own understanding. Embrace the simple instruction to love. My word tells you in multiple ways what is expected of you. Just follow those instructions.

Leave your heart in my hands. That is what you do when you choose love—when you choose me. And the joy that will fill you will be like a warm embrace, overwhelming and overcoming the difficulties and problems of life. I promise. Rejoice!

(When all else fails, read the instructions!)

Proverbs 3:5-6; I Chronicles 16:27

8

If you, my child, are hurting for the few whom you know are suffering and dealing with difficulties in their lives, how much more do you think I suffer for mankind? Life on earth could be so much simpler for so many but for the choices they make. It is my wish and my will that my children choose me. That choice does not bring ease, but it does bring peace and joy. It brings a restful spirit—a heart filled with love. The "feelings" of this world cannot compare to what I can do in the life of one of my children.

Choose each day which way you will go—the way of the world or the way of your father.

I am the way. I promise. Rejoice!

Joshua 24:15; II John 1:4

9

As you go, as you work, as you think, as you rest—remember me. Let me walk with you, work with you, rest with you, guide your mind and your heart. Leave all to me and you will be blessed.

Those who labor and are heavy-laden should turn to me and turn over their burdens to me. I am able to carry your burdens and your woes. Look to me as your helper in *all* things. Turn to me in every situation. Why do you resist me? Have I not shown myself to be faithful? Do you not see my hand in your life? Why is it so hard for you to trust me? Why, child?

Let go of those burdens. Release your anger. Put aside your heartaches. You can trust me. I promise. Rejoice!

Deuteronomy 8:18-19

10

Streaks of sunlight, the call of birds, the cool morning, the gentle breeze—all quiet indications that I am present.

I am here to listen to the cries of your heart, here to soothe your troubled soul, here to heal your broken heart, here to calm your active mind, here to heal your aching body, here to hear and answer your prayers, here to show you love and peace and joy. Here. Close. Always. I promise. Rejoice!

Psalm 10:17

11

I send my words to you in many ways. You must be open to receive my messages. When all seems dark...when all seems beyond your strength to endure...when all goes awry...trust me. It is easy to trust and be positive in the good times, but questions arise when things get tough. What you must always remember is that I am here, at hand. Close enough to fill your every need. I have not abandoned you. Your well-being is important to me. Have I not *always* kept you close? Have I not *always* given you *more* than the desires of your heart? And so shall it continue to be.

Do what is honest. Do what is pure. Do what is true. Live according to my instructions for your life, and you will see my hand in every situation and in your future days.

Do not doubt. Have faith in me, in my ability to work miracles, and in my love for you.

Though life's storm is swirling around you, remember that I am the *eye* of the storm, and in that *eye* you will find my peace and, yes, even my joy! I promise!!! Rejoice!

Psalm 24:3-4; Psalm 107:29

12

Distractions and frustrations are not at fault, child, when you stay away from time with me. Your own choices are at fault. Do not look for excuses. Instead, look for reasons to be near me. Set aside a time and a place for me. Life on earth is not perfect. You can feel closer to me in some locations more than in others. But that is not reason enough to ignore our ability to have time together.

I am always close, always waiting, looking forward to times of communion with you. I do not leave you—you are the one who turns your back on me. I love you. I am present. I am omnipresent. I promise. Rejoice!

Numbers 6:26; Colossians 2:5

13

Fresh and new are my words to you, but they are "tried and true" as well. My message is the same, but it becomes fresh for you as you are able to ingest and taste each word. I am here. I always have been here, and I always will be here. Here to guide and direct. Here to love and comfort. Here to chastise. Here to teach. Fresh and new. Tried and true. Lessons—for you.

I want you to understand that you must continue to trust and believe. I want you to continue to love. Choose faith. Choose compassion. Choose to spend time with me. Choose my way over the way of the world. Be patient, though it may be difficult. Choose not worry, but instead choose hope. That *hope* will prove in your life to bring all that you need.

Recite "enough" as a mantra. I am enough. Always and forever. Yea, though you go through dark valleys, I am the sunshine peeping over the ridge. Enough. I promise. Rejoice!

Jeremiah 30:2 (The Message): "Write everything I tell you in a book."

14

Lay all at my feet and walk away. That is so hard for my children, but you must do it. Worrying, fretting, and revisiting hurts and pains and failures does no good for your life. Each moment is a new beginning for you—a new opportunity to follow me.

So lay down the burdens, the baggage of life that you are dragging along. Lay them before me. I am able to carry those burdens for you. I am the "porter." You can walk on from this point feeling "lighter" and freer. I am your burden bearer. I am your savior. I am your guide. I am the great *I am*. I promise. Rejoice!

Matthew 6:25-26

15

Fear God. Do what he tells you. (Ecclesiastes 12:13)

When you hear the words "fear God," you should translate that as "respect" or "stand in awe of." Fear of God is not a negative emotion, but a positive one. Inherent in the word "fear" is a call to put aside your worldly ways and listen for God's call to you, his will for your life, his desire to help you stay on the path that is right for you. Listen for his words to you. Be aware of his presence in all of your life. Stand strong and be faithful. God is good. He wants good for you. He has promised.

I do not want quivering servants. I want strong, courageous children who seek my face and strive to follow my ways. I am a loving God. I promise. Rejoice!

16

"I need thee every hour."[13] Remember the words of the hymn, but also realize that as you have need of me, so also do I have need of you. Enticing distractions are always appearing—some good, some not good. But you must *decide* to make time for me and for our time together.

Your heart may suffer "blows"—pain inflicted by others. Your good name may be disparaged in ways you know not. But through it all, I am present. I may not "fix" problems in the way you might like. I did not even fix my own problems when I was on the earth. Men spoke all manner of evil against me.

Can you find comfort knowing that you have my unconditional love? Can you accept my peace for you, even when your joy disappears? Can you *believe*, truly believe, that I am with you, and that my love for you and my care for you extend beyond the boundaries of your imagination? It is true. I am enough—for all circumstances and all situations. I bring love and compassion and healing to your anxious, hurting life. I am always here…always with you…always. I promise. Rejoice!

Psalm 23:4-5

17

Though waking or sleeping, I am with you. My words are flowing to you. Open your spirit to enable it to be able to receive me. I am blessing and life for my children. I am substance and sustenance for your lives.

The cares of your heart are all heard by me. I am answering your prayers. Listen for my voice. Watch for my working without ceasing on your behalf.

I am love and compassion. When your tears form, I am there to catch them before they fall. I am with you always—even to the very ends of the earth. I promise. Rejoice!

Ephesians 1:3-14

18

Listen, listen—that is the secret. My children want to talk with me. I do not mind, but I, too, have wisdom to share, and that requires a listening heart. Listen for my words. Listen for my voice. I still speak to my children. I never stopped speaking. I promise. Rejoice!

James 1:22-25

19

Trust me. Consider all of the world that surrounds you. Do the birds and mammals seem to fret and worry about their futures? No. Yes, they do have feelings—of fear, of contentment. But they move about without anxiety for their futures. You must do the same. They make preparation. The squirrels store food. The bears prepare to hibernate. They do what I have charged them to do. So should you.

Take my charges to you seriously. Prepare your hearts and minds to be faithful followers. Turn to me for all things. Leave behind all worry and all anxiety.

You are concerned about situations and circumstances. I am concerned about your presence in eternity.

Think on my words, my promises. Believe and have faith in me. Put aside selfishness and focus on me. Your life will become a reflection of my presence.

When your light "shines," it is a reflection of my spirit within you. That light will make a difference in this world in which you live. I promise. Rejoice!

Luke 12:24-26

20

What better way for your mind and heart to be turned away from me than for you to concentrate on the ways others have brought hurt into your life? Your thoughts lead to defending yourself and your "good" name. Take no thought of those evil things. Instead, turn your mind and your heart to me. I am true love and light. I am peace and joy. The unkind words and deeds of others are not for eternity, but I am with you for eternity.

With your whole being, concentrate on me. With your whole heart, accept my love for you. Know that I mean good for you, even when others may not. Pray for those who persecute you. Think of how much they need me in their lives. Pray for the same good to come to them that you desire in your own life. These are opportunities for you to find grace. Embrace the opportunities, and you will always find me faithful. I promise. Rejoice!

III John 1:11; Romans 12:12-18

21

I am a faithful father. I am a God of miracles. Think about this. Even today, people are trying to explain away the miracle of the parting of the Red Sea. But does it matter? What matters is that I, your Father and your God, saved my people with just the miracle they needed, just when they needed it. Think on this. Ponder this.

I am. That means that I am here for you, to care for you. I am still the God of miracles. When you need me, I am here. Always. So never worry or fret or fear, because I am faithful.

Child, you must learn to trust me. I am worthy of your trust. I promise. Rejoice!

Hebrews 2:4: Revelation 1:8

22

Praise God, from whom all blessings flow. Praise God, all creatures here below. Praise God above, ye heavenly hosts. Praise Father, Son and Holy Ghost. Amen.

Praise. It is truly "music to my ears." To hear my children praise me means to me that they *know* me. They understand that I am the Father, the Creator, the Healer, the Comforter, the Provider. It speaks of a relationship with me.

Praise not only brings joy to the Father, but it also lightens the burden of my children. When you praise me, there is no room for self-pity and anger and frustration and doubt. Praise wells up inside you and overcomes the negative.

So sing out your praises with joy in your hearts. Joy is a powerful gift from me, and praise is a wonderful gift from you. I promise. Rejoice!

Psalm 13:6; I Peter 1:3-5

23

People, situations, ideas and thoughts pass through your mind and your life for a reason. There is nothing haphazard in my creation. Rather than becoming numb and oblivious to these people and thoughts, ask me why they are in your life and what you should do about them.

Perhaps you need to lift a prayer on their behalf. Perchance there is something physical you can provide for them. Maybe you can share an encouraging word.

My ways are not your ways. Your challenge is to align your earthly life with my heavenly one. Watch the blessings flow when you do so. They will. I promise. Rejoice!

III John 1:2; James 5:16; I Thessalonians 5:17

24

Fresh breezes. Cool air. Birdsong. Sunshine. All these remind you of my presence. I am creator. The changing of the leaves in the fall, the rotation of the seasons, are all a part of my plan for this earthly home of yours and should indicate to you that I have a plan for your lives.

You struggle to hold on to what you know, but I am showing you an ever-changing, ever-unfolding miracle. Think on this. If I can unfold wonders in nature, why would I fail to unfold miracles in your life?

Instead of fretting about a future you cannot see, just rest in me. Turn to me. Acknowledge me. Recognize me, and trust. I am a trustworthy father.

My love for you far outweighs any anxiety or fear you may have for your future. Trust me and my love and care for you. When you do this, you will be amazed at what happens in your life. I promise. Rejoice!

Acts 2:22

25

I never cease to be surprised when my own are startled at the answers to their prayers. Do you believe? Do you trust me? Then why are you filled with wonder at answered prayer? I am your faithful father. I hear and I answer. Try with your all to see the answers to your prayers, and be thankful. That is difficult for my children, for even as you are "thankful," you are allowing your mind to wander to all those requests that remain unanswered.

My ways are not your ways. My answers come in many forms. You do not always recognize the answers, and they are not always *your* answers. This is why you must trust and believe. *You* may never see my answers, but you are called to continuously believe and trust and be thankful. I am faithful. I promise. Rejoice!

I John 3:23-24; James 1:6-8

26

You are worried and anxious about many things. You try with your earthly ways to ignore these concerns, but they are there and they build a barrier between us—you and me.

Your worries reveal a lack of trust and therefore a lack of peace. Is this the sort of life you think I have planned for you?

My plans are for peace. My plans are for a spirit-led life for you. When you allow others, or circumstances, to enter and to interfere, then peace is hidden from you. My peace is accessible, but you, my child, have blinded yourself to it.

Take off the blinders! Choose to put worries aside. That's right... *choose!* Make a conscious decision. Trust me that I hear and answer your prayers. Turn from sin (from missing my will for you) and turn toward grateful obedience.

Peace will reign. Joy will flow. Prayers will be answered in ways you dare not dream. I promise. Rejoice!

Numbers 6:26; Psalm 29:11

27

Surely I am with you always, even unto the ends of the earth. Carry this thought—this promise—with you as you go through the day ahead.

Not only am I with you in the present moment, but also I go before you, behind you, beside you, below you, above you and within you every moment, and with every step. I promise. Rejoice!

Matthew 28:20

28

Lo, I am with you always, even unto the ends of the earth. Every step of the way, I am with you. There is nowhere you can go where I am not found. So why do you worry? Why are you anxious for the future? Leave all to me, and ease your troubled mind. In *all*, trust me.

My children know the right things to do but do not always follow the path I have set before them. I tell you that I have prepared the way for you. I am waiting for each of you to turn to me. I will walk with you. I will carry you when you are too weak to take a step. I am always with you.

So put aside the worry. Put aside the fretting. Put aside fears for the future. Instead, ask me what I have for you to do this moment—this day. And as you learn to trust in the moment, the worries will fall away and peace will reign in your hearts.

Others will see your peace and will seek me. So go forth this day trusting me, depending on me, and feel the peace descend on your spirit and in your life. Believe. Trust. Obey. I am with you always. I promise. Rejoice!

Matthew 28:20; Luke 1:79b

29

Do good to those whose lives intersect your own. Do not focus on the times you are treated with unkindness, but instead repay the unkindness with compassion. Try to see people as I see them. Each is my child. I love each person in my creation.

Everyone sins and falls short of my best for them. That does not cause me to withhold my love from them. Can you do the same?

In my word, I tell you to love the unlovely, to turn the other cheek. Practice this. Try repaying unkindness with kindness. Do not judge another child of my kingdom. Do not waste your moments nursing hurts and anger. Instead, turn them over to me. I can handle all.

Your role is to love all of humanity. That includes loving those who do wrong and who have wronged you or hurt you. Put aside your hurts. Ask me for help if it feels too difficult for you. I can help you love. I can help you overcome sin and evil. I am love. I promise. Rejoice!

I Peter 3:11-13; Hebrews 13:16

30

To my children who dwell in the twilight (not quite in the dark, not quite in the sun), I say: Open your eyes to the light. Open your spirit to the light of my presence, and allow me to shine on you and within you.

You fear the exposure of your sins, but you have no idea of the blessings that flow from my light in your life. Let my light so shine that all will see it, recognize me and glorify me in my heaven. Blessings will flow when you allow me fully into your life. I promise. Rejoice!

I John 2:9-10; I John 1:7

31

Open your heart today to me, your father. Open your spirit. Try listening for my "voice" each moment of this day. Look, at every turn, for signs of my leading. This is "practice."

Practice my presence all day. When your mind tries to take you away from me and my desires for you, turn back to the pathway along which I am leading you. This will be a conscious effort on your part. Your mind will be engaged. You will learn a discipline through this practice of staying close to me.

Practice my presence. You will uncover treasures of blessings along the way. I promise. Rejoice!

Revelation 3:20

Life Guide
NOVEMBER

1

Set aside worry and fretting and heartache. Set aside all negative thoughts and fears. Set aside anything that takes you away from the conscious recognition of my presence with you.

All these emotions are self-motivated. So set aside self. That is what I mean for you to do every moment of every day. Push back all thoughts that are selfishly tinged and substitute thoughts of me instead. Ask me what I would have you think, what I would have you do. Focus your thoughts and attentions outside yourself, and greater blessings than you can imagine will come your way.

You, yourself, are the biggest hindrance and barrier to what I want to do in your life. Step aside and watch me work in your life. I will. I promise. Rejoice!

Colossians 3:9-10; Romans 6:6

2

Sometimes you must do things you do not want to do, and sometimes you must go where you do not want to go. Put aside your resistance during these times and put your trust in me.

I am not just a good friend who walks beside you, available at your whims. I am your Heavenly Father. I am a powerful and ever-present force. God. *I am.*

Trust me with your life. Yea, trust me with your soul. Our spirits are linked. I have chosen you as my child, and you have acknowledged me as your father. This relationship is unlike any earthly relationship you know. I understand your unbelief, your hesitations. But I tell you, my child, they are unfounded.

Put all in my care. I care for you as no other does or can. I promise. Rejoice!

Psalm 9:10; Psalm 20:7; Nahum 1:7

3

When the need within you for my presence is so great, write it down. I do not need it, but you do. Seek me every moment, and you will find me. Ask, and you will receive my answers. Stay close. Always, stay close to me. My children are precious to me, and I do not leave them. I promise. Rejoice!

Amos 5:4-6a

4

Be alert! Look for my leadings this day. Keep your eyes open to see where I will lead you. Listen to your heart. Be silent until I nudge you to speak. Trust me in all things. I am faithful.

You have seen my faithfulness in answered prayers. Now, praise me and thank me for all that I have done and all that I will do. Stay close to me. Practice resting in my presence. I will always be with you. I promise. Rejoice!

II Samuel 2:6a; Jeremiah 6:16a

5

Just as my rain refreshes the earth, so does my spirit refresh your spirit. Turn your heart to me this day and allow my holy rain to wash away worry, anxiety and fear. Rivers of change may face you, but I am the captain of the ship of life, and I am able to steer you through dangerous and difficult currents into peaceful waters and abundant life. I promise. Rejoice!

Jeremiah 31:25

6

Through me all things are possible. When you refuse to embrace this fact, this *truth*, then you are exhibiting a lack of trust—a lack of faith.

Cling to my promises. Think back on all the ways I have been faithful to answer your prayers. Embrace me. Believe in me. Trust me. I will not fail you. In fact, when you lay your concerns at my feet and leave them there, earth cannot imagine the blessings I have in store for you. I promise. Rejoice!

Matthew 19:26

7

I am the Lord, and there is no other. (Isaiah 45:5)

Though my word "roars" at you sometimes, I am a gentle and loving father. You, my child, wander away and need my discipline, but also my love and compassion. In times of anxiety and uncertainty, I call you to remember and to trust me. Remember all the times you have turned to me and all the ways I have faithfully answered your prayers, and be thankful.

Choose this season to remember and to give thanks to me for all that is good. Choose to trust. Choose to believe that I am the Lord, and there is no other. I promise. Rejoice!

8

Rest in me. Do you think that means to lie down and take a nap? *No!* It means to allow the tensions to be released from your body—those tensions that are a strong indication that *you* are trying to handle life all alone.

Be aware of the tensions and release them. Let them go. *Rest* in me. Then get moving, allowing me to walk you forward into the choices I have for you, into the life I have chosen for you.

It is a life of blessing, a life of compassion, a life of giving and receiving, a life of love. Trust me. Allow me to lead you into paths of peace. I am able to do all things. I promise. Rejoice!

Matthew 11:29

9

And God said, "Let there be light…" Do you think that means the sun and the moon? No. I was speaking of the light of my presence in this world.

On gray days (both physically and emotionally), you tend to languish and wane. On sunny days, you seem to brighten in your spirit, and that brightness spills out of you. This is an example of my light within you. When you are filled with the light of my holy spirit, you share that light in every word, in every deed, and even in silence (through the glow you present to the world). You cannot hold it in. It flows through you to all whom you meet.

So let your light so shine before men that they will see me and glorify my Father in Heaven. When you do this, blessings will flow and nearly overwhelm you. I promise. Rejoice!

Genesis 1:3

10

The earth is the Lord's. The glorious colors you admire in fall are all a part of my plan. Sleeping and waking. All of nature participates.

My word reminds you of the sparrow and how I have provided for it. Even so have I done in nature. From the falling leaves that warm the roots of my plants to the coursing of renewal through branches in the spring, so it is with my children. I have ordered this life so that you have times of rest and times of activity. Honor my plan. Listen for my instruction. Stand ready to serve, and gratefully accept my rest times for you.

My plans for you are good. I promise. Rejoice!

Genesis 1:1; Psalm 8:9

11

Praise me as a little child praises me—with joyful exuberance! Praise me for the little things as well as the big things. Praise me as you go.

You will find that each experience becomes fuller with joy and blessings, each sight more beautiful, and each person more dear. I promise! Rejoice!

Exodus 15:2; Deuteronomy 32:3-4

12

Gently, gently comes the day—sometimes with raindrops, sometimes with rays of sunshine. Embrace the day you are given. Start each day with me. Start by listening for my soft and gentle voice, leading you forward. Find your Bethel—your quiet place of prayer and communion.

Stop your active mind and ceaseless motion long enough to be grateful for the moments you have, and long enough to hear my words of instruction and blessing for you.

Gently proceed into your day, and acknowledge my presence at every turn. Quietly give thanks. In turn, your gentle spirit will spread my love and joy all around you as you go. I promise. Rejoice!

Luke 4:42a

13

This is a time of remembrance. It is important for you to remember and to think back on all that I have done in your life, and all that I have been. You must remember the ways I have gone before you. You should reflect upon all the answered prayers that have come your way. Sometimes there have been answers to prayers that have not yet found words to form them. I am at work in your life. I am always answering, always leading, always guiding, always finding solutions for you—not in *your* time, but in my time. You must believe these things, and the best way to make sure that your belief is strong is to remember.

I told my people of old to remember me—to even wear on their foreheads remembrances of me. It is no different for you. Do you believe? Do you trust me? Do you think that I am able to do all things at just the right time, in just the right way? You must sit at my feet and let your tears of gratitude fall as you thank me for all the answers of your past.

Then, child, look forward, believing in me and in all that I have planned for you. And be grateful. I am your Father and your God. I can do all things that you can imagine and many more that you cannot even fathom. Believe in me, and the desires of your heart will materialize before you. I promise. Rejoice and rejoice!

Luke 22:19; Deuteronomy 8:18

14

Come to me early or come to me late. Just come. Come and sit quietly, and wait for me. Listen for a still, small voice, a stirring in your spirit. Learn to recognize me, and learn to listen.

I have placed you under my wings. You are safe. All your worries and concerns are being addressed. You have trusted my faithfulness. Continue to pray and trust. You are safe. You are loved.

Repent from your own unloving ways. Be still and silent, even when it is difficult to do so. Do not allow the insincerity and ugliness of others to corrupt your heart and mind.

Practice my presence. Listen for my voice. You are safe. I promise. Rejoice!

I Corinthians 1:7; Acts 3:19

15

Oh ye of little faith. Do you not realize that I hear your prayers? Have you not yet learned that I have a plan for your life? Do you not recognize me as the great provider? Can you not trust me to care for all your needs?

Taste and see that I am good. Acknowledge the many ways I answer your prayers. Praise me in my sanctuary. Thank me all the day long, for I am your Father and your God, and I love you. I promise. Rejoice!

Matthew 8:26; Matthew 17:20

16

Truly, I am doing great works of which you know not. I know the hurts before you experience them. I know the attitudes before you see them manifested. I am working in this world to build a platform of love. There are those who seek to tear down or ignore my work, my presence. Sometimes their destruction is intentional, but often it is not. Some are my enemies, and some are my own children who seek to destroy the good I intend for all. They know not what they do.

You must not concentrate on the problems. You must acknowledge those problems and hand them all over to me. I am sufficient. I am willing to take care of all that troubles you. Do not fret. Do not worry. Practice love. You are not responsible for fixing the problems of others. You must concentrate instead on your relationship with me—your father. I can handle the rest. I promise. Rejoice!

II Corinthians 7:4; Psalm 37:1, 7

17

Jeremiah 29:10-14

Yes, I give you verses from my word to cling to…to encourage you… to guide you…to give you hope. I am true to my word. Believe. Hope. Pray. Be confident in me.

As you go about your day, remember that nothing I do is without purpose or in vain. Believe me. Pray for those with whom you find your-selves. Lift up people and situations to me. Be faithful to daily turn to me, and you will see the answers to your prayers, and you will know my presence with you. I promise. Rejoice!

18

When the "heaviness" of the world weighs you down, I am here. When joy floats your spirits, I am here. When you trod through your day, think-ing you are OK and don't need to bother me, I am still here, waiting to commune with you. I am with you always. I promise. Rejoice!

Luke 15:31; Isaiah 59:21

19

Each new day holds promises for my children. Look at this day as an unfolding adventure.

Do not embrace the thoughts of "boring" or "inactive." Instead, look to me for guidance. I will show you through the adventure of this day, one step at a time. I promise. Rejoice!

Psalm 25:5; John 16:13

20

A day of change, a day of reflection. When change comes into your life, my child, it is good to reflect on how I have been with you in the past. It is good to remember your times of desolation and your times of joy. It is good for you to remember how I, your father, have been with you. Do you see my mark on your life?

Contemplate this. Think on nature and how the ripples on a lake can indicate the presence of one of my creatures—a bug, a fish, a turtle. You do not see these creatures *necessarily*, but you can see the result of their presence. So it is in your life, and so I want it to be.

You nor others can see me, but you can see the evidence of my presence with you.

Praise me for all that I have done, am doing and will do. Praise me for answered prayers. Praise me for my constancy and my faithfulness. For I am ever with you, loving you, revealing myself to you. I promise. Rejoice!

James 1:17; Exodus 33:14

21

Your job for this day is to seek me at every turn. Allow my presence and my voice to enter into each part of your day. Shower love and joy on all you meet.

Go forth in joy. Be a smile someone needs. Be a listening ear to help another who has burdens to share. Be my servant and my child, and I will not leave you nor forsake you. I promise. Rejoice!

Psalm 119:10; Psalm 5:11

22

You tend to think of rainy days as lacking the sun, but you "know" the sun is just behind those clouds.

So it is in life. When you have dark, cloudy days—days of storms and troubles—the *son* is behind those clouds, just waiting for you to acknowledge his presence.

I am here. Always. Waiting for you to come to me. I am stronger than those storms and brighter than those cloudy days. I promise. Rejoice!

Psalm 107:29-31

23

Do not grow weary of doing the "right" things—those things I lead you to do. Find joy and peace in the opportunities I am sending your way to serve. You will bring joy to others through serving as I direct, but the joy will be multiplied when you rebuke weariness and let my light shine through you. I promise. Rejoice!

Hebrews 12:3; Isaiah 40:30-31

24

Joyful, joyful, we adore thee, God of glory, Lord of light.

I am the Lord of light and of glory. Worship me today with this in mind.

You sometimes fail to remember my majesty. I am the creator of the universe, the Father and God of all. You get familiar with me as we converse, and that is as it should be. But I also want you to remember who *I am*. I am God.

Adore me with praise and joy. Live a grateful, thankful life. Let a song of joy and thanksgiving and praise resonate in your days and in your nights. Remember my goodness and remember my majesty.

I am the *one constant* in all of the universe. I promise. Rejoice!

I Chronicles 16:27-29; Jude 1:25

25

My times are not your times, nor are my ways your ways. Taste and see that I am good. Know beyond any doubt that I am God—your Father.

So trust me, even when situations are uncomfortable or do not seem "right" in your eyes. Trust me when there are "desert" experiences in your life—when I may seem to be far away. Trust me.

I am always nearer than you perceive. I am always working for good for those who love me and for those who seek me with their whole heart.

I am near. I am present. I am love. I am solutions. I am creative. I am powerful. I am God. I promise. Rejoice!

Psalm 34:8; Revelation 1:8

26

Let the sunlight of my presence permeate even the rainiest of days. Let the warm memories of my presence with you overcome the chill of the world. Let me flourish in your life so that you become overcomers—so that you, like me, can overcome the weighty influences present in the world and live lives in my light and my joy.

I came into the world to help you overcome self and to help you make choices that join our spirits for eternity. You can feel easily overwhelmed in your circumstances, but when you call on me, I am waiting—at hand—to be your helper.

Believe in me, in my presence with you. Believe in my faithfulness to help you be an overcomer. Believe in my truth and my light and my spirit. Believe that all things can work together for good. Believe that I am with you always. Believe, and this truth—God—will set you free. I promise. Rejoice!

I John 4:4; Romans 12:21

27

Let not your heart be troubled. The understanding of the world and its people is for me and not for you. You are to love me and share that love with all you meet. When your love and sharing are rebuffed, then walk away. But continue to pray, and, through me, send love to that person.

You cannot solve the world's problems, nor can you resolve the woes of its people. No. That is for me. You are called to love and to pray. Leave the rest in my hands and at my feet. I am able. I promise. Rejoice!

Proverbs 23:17-18

28

My child, I am here. Turn your heart and eyes to me. I never leave you, but you often fail to recognize my presence. Wait! Wait on my nudging today, and you will have such a sense of my presence. I promise. Rejoice!

Acts 26:18

29

A call to prayer. A call to giving. A call to open your life to others. A call to be open in your life to what others may offer you—criticism, suggestions, information, guidance, love, compassion.

Receive the call and discern my presence in those around you. I will be with you. I promise. Rejoice!

Psalm 17:6

30

Listen. Comprehend. Share love with all who surround you. Isn't that what people want from me? Why would they not need the same from you? In this way, you can make a difference in this world in which you are placed. Do you think you are here by chance? No. You are here to further my kingdom—not by great and mighty works, but by daily devotion to my guidance. Listen. Comprehend. Share. Love. Rejoice!

Matthew 4:17; James 2:5; Romans 14:17-19; Colossians 1:9-13

Life Guide

DECEMBER

1

For safety and protection
—for love and care
—for direction and discernment
—for your blessings
I am thankful.

Go forth and continue to be thankful. I am with you, even amidst the noise and distractions that surround you. I am here. I am love. I am enough. I promise. Rejoice!

Colossians 3:15

2

I abide with you, child. I am in the here and now. I am past, present and future. I am in heaven and in earth. I am your father and your friend. I am all that you need. Take your eyes off your earthly problems and focus on me. Look to me instead of to others for help, and I will show you the pathway to follow. I will make the way straight for you. I will be your strength when you are weak.

I have gifts for you—gifts of joy and peace and love. Embrace these gifts, and do not unwrap the false offerings before you—anger, resentment and bitterness. I realize that life can be difficult. I never promised otherwise. But I have promised to be with you and to love and sustain you. Read my word. Listen for my voice. I am at hand.

I promise. Rejoice!

Psalm 91:1; Hebrews 2:4

3

Today is a new day—a fresh start, an unmarked page. Look with fresh eyes all around you. Be encouraged by the consistency of my presence in this world I have created. Be sure that I am your Lord and Father. Leave behind sadness and worry and look to this day—the day ahead. Here is your opportunity to stop fretting about the past or the future and to live fully in each moment.

Relish joy. Give love. Be compassionate. Remain open to see and to do my will, and if you do, you will sense my presence all around you. You will become more keenly aware of me and my love for my children. Open yourself up to the promises of this day. You will not be disappointed.

I promise. Rejoice!

Song of Songs 2:11-13; Psalm 119:148

4

Fret not. Worry not, my child, for I am come that you might have abundant life. A life filled with love and peace. A life lacking in nothing. A life lived on this earth so that others can come to know me through you. That is my desire for you. So open your arms and heart to embrace all the good and marvelous gifts I have for you. Take comfort that your troubles are only for a season. Remember that joy comes in the morning, and that with joy also comes a deeper relationship with me, your Heavenly Father.

I am love and peace and joy and protection and provision. You need not worry. I promise. Rejoice!

Romans 5:17; Psalm 42:4

5

Child, you are in this place for a reason. Cherish the people in your life. Cherish the love that flows. I am walking with you on this path. I bring you goodness and blessings. I bring you love and companionship. I bring you joy and peace. Embrace these gifts from me. Share these gifts with others. The greatest of these gifts is *love*. I am love. I am meant to be shared. I am meant to be your friend and your companion. I am all things. I am found wherever you gaze. I am omnipresent. I promise. Rejoice!

III John 1:4; Jude 1:2

6

For the glory of this life, thank me. One day you will realize how precious these days have been. You go on and on with the minutiae of life, forgetting to follow me, taking up your own sword of anger and discontent. Leave the fighting to me. I have ordered and ordained a life of peace and joy for you. Why do you insist on your own ways rather than my ways? I am truth and life and love and joy and peace.

Do not be discouraged, my child. Do not lean on your own understanding. Trust me. Turn to me. I am waiting and willing to handle every care and concern in your life. Trust. I am always faithful. I promise. Rejoice!

John 12:26; II Chronicles 32:7a

7

Surely the presence of the Lord is in this place. We need your presence, Father. We need you in every situation. We need to know you are with us—round about us. We need your healing. We need your direction. We need you. Come and be near us, and help us draw near to you, I pray.

I never leave you or forsake you, my child. I am ever present. I am only waiting for your spirit to be attuned to mine. Then we can communicate. Then you will *know* beyond any doubt that I am with you. You must make the effort to quiet your mind and open your heart. I am waiting. I am always waiting. I am always here for you. I promise. Rejoice!

Deuteronomy 31:8

8

Relax in me. *Rest* in me. Why do you assume that the problems you face in life are yours alone to bear? Why can you not let me carry your burden of cares? Why don't you trust me? Release the load that wears you down, and allow me to walk beside you and carry that load for you. Feel the lightness of relinquishment, even now. Trust. Have faith. Believe. I am able to do all things—and so are you—when and *only* when you rest in me. I promise. Rejoice!

II Corinthians 12:9

9

Be still, my child, still and waiting, as if you were a shepherd on a hillside. Allow my peace to descend on your soul—on your spirit, which is joined with my spirit. Allow love to flow through you. Allow that love to continue to flow outward. Think less of your own troubles and problems and more of the woes of others. Choose to love your family, your friends, your neighbors, and humankind. Choose love.

Follow my lead. Follow my nudgings. Follow me. And I, your father, will watch over you, protect you, guide you, and only allow into your life what you can bear. I am always with you. I promise. Rejoice!

II Peter 1:5-8

10

May God bless my coming and my going, my thoughts and my words, my actions, my gifts, my very being, on this earth and beyond.

I do bless you, my child. It is my pleasure to bless my children. Open your eyes to my blessings, which fall all around you like soft and gentle flakes of snow. Embrace these blessings. Use them for yourself and for others. Whatever you do for others will come back to you tenfold. I am God of plenty and of love. I do not give miserly gifts. I promise. Rejoice!

Numbers 6:24-26

11

Slipping through your fingers like grains of sand is time as you know it. But you cannot fathom time as I know it. Do not worry and fret about your time on this earth, or your lack thereof. Leave your worries with me. I am leading and guiding you every moment, every day. You need to "mark" time. I enjoy eternity. Time as you know it will cease, and you will come to know eternity, too. I promise. Rejoice!

Psalm 34:15

12

I have been waiting for you. Sit with me. Trust me. In this day and in the ones ahead, remember me in all things. Be thankful to me. Be gracious to others. Love without withholding. Blessings beyond measure will shower on you and on your loved ones. I promise. Rejoice!

I Peter 3:4; I Thessalonians 4:11a

13

The face you present to the world can easily be misunderstood. You often are not perceived in the way you intend.

And so, my child, my directive to you is to seek me in all things. Ask me to go before you. Ask me to so fill you that others truly see me in your eyes and in your conduct.

You cannot do this under your own strength. You can only do it with my help, my intervention. Pray for me to go before you, behind you, beside you, above you, below you, within you, in all things and through all circumstances. When you do this consistently, continually, others will recognize the spirit of God that is in you. I promise. Rejoice!

Jeremiah 29:13; Amos 5:4

14

Set aside time for me. Choose to stop your everyday activities and wait for me. I am at hand. My kingdom waits for you. You need this time of quietness. You need this time to be with me.

I need this time with you as well. Blessings will flow, and you will recognize me in the midst of your circumstances. I am always here, but you will recognize me because your heart will be attuned to my spirit. Blessings will flow. I promise. Rejoice!

Exodus 14:14

15

(Read Isaiah 45.)

"I will go before you and level the exalted places" (v. 2a). "Turn to me and be saved…for I am God, and there is no other" (v. 22).

The things of this earth that you enjoy are all my creations. Light and love are all from me. I created the earth and all that dwells within it. So turn to me. I am God, and there is no other.

Do not be distracted by those people and things that would keep your focus from me. Do not allow anger to rear its ugliness in your life. Say "no" to judging others or situations. Choose love. Be love in this place where you reside. Allow my spirit to be strong in your life. Anger and disdain are not from me. Love and compassion are from me. Turn away from evil, but not before sending a prayer for good toward the evil you encounter.

You will always be disappointed by people, but I will never disappoint. I will never betray. I am love and joy and peace.

Rest in the comfort of my presence, and allow me to teach you and to lead you. For this is the path I have for you. I promise. Rejoice!

16

Though times are tough and hopes are waning, I am faithful. Though you look through tears, I am found. Though you despair, I bring hope and joy. Turn to me. Sit with me. Listen for my still, small voice. There is no need for fear and despair. I am here. I am hearing the cries of your heart. I am stilling your fears. I am setting out the course you should follow. Listen. Heed. Believe. Praise me. Love me. I am your faithful father. I promise. Rejoice!

Psalm 86:2-4; John 10:27

17

You have been through the valley, but I have been with you for every moment of that journey. You have had your conscious thoughts consumed by circumstances, but I have been king of your unconscious thoughts. Stay now on the path of prayer, and you will see my victory in the flesh. You will know my answered prayer, and gratitude will flood your heart. I promise. Rejoice!

Psalm 23:4

18

Trust...trust...trust. When people and circumstances and situations scream at you to doubt, trust...trust...trust. All is well. I promise. Rejoice!

Psalm 9:10; Psalm 20:7; Proverbs 3:5; Isaiah 12:2

19

(The following listening was done by my daughter, Anna Taylor Freeman, and shared here with her permission.)

Hear me over all of the distractions. Seek me. Your life will never settle enough for you to hear me. Work. I am here. I am always here. The cloudiness in your eyes—in your heart—will clear when you seek me and find me in the busyness of your day. I never promised that leisure would bring peace. You must find peace in spite of the hectic days, in the middle of the hectic days. Carry it with you. Offer it to others. Be my peace. I am not security. I am calm. I am the calm in life's storms. Share me. Love me above all others, above all things. Do this, and I will provide.

(Today I pray for each of us that we can be God's peace—in spite of the fears, anxieties, stresses, errands, tasks, etc. I love you each to the moon and back!!)

Numbers 6:26

20

A spirit of fear is not from me. You must believe this and trust me, child. When the things of your life seem in disarray, when you feel out of control and out of sorts, you must trust me and believe (against all the world's voices that shout to you) in me. I am love.

How can love operate if not in the best interest of my children? What you *think* to be best for you is often flawed thinking. I know what is best for you, and if you will quiet your mind and trust, I will answer all your prayers—in my time.

Trust. Believe. Pray. Rest. I am answering all. I promise. Rejoice!

II Timothy 1:7; Romans 8:15

21

When my people, who are called by my name, join together in prayer to me, it is a powerful force.

I hear your prayers as they petition me, but the power of joined hearts in prayer is more an encouragement for you, my children. You feel the comfort and you need the undergirding that the prayers of others bring.

So take comfort when others join you in prayer and when they lift you in prayer to me. But remember always that I hear every whisper of petition from your heart. I promise. Rejoice!

Leviticus 26:12; II Chronicles 7:14-15

22

Bad weather or good, I am with you. Sun, rain, snow, ice, clouds—I am always here. When your hearts are overflowing with joy or sadness, I am present. When you feel in control and when you do not—still, I am here.

Relinquish your need to control to me. Step back after dropping your concerns and heartaches at my feet. This is trust. First you ask, then you step back, then you believe that I am able to do all things that you have requested of me.

Be very sure of my presence. Be very certain of my love. Be comforted in the sheer fact that *you* do not have control, but that *I do*. I am. That means everything. Trust. Obey. Leave it all with me. I am able. I promise. Rejoice!

Colossians 1:16-20

23

Sun, clouds, wind, rain, storms, simple breezes—all of these are part of life. Do you notice that there might be more inclement times than sunny days? Just remember through it all that I am with you—ever present, omniscient, offering you unconditional love. Remind yourself in *all* these times of my presence with you. Remind yourself to continue your communication with me. I desire your love just as much as you desire mine. I promise. Rejoice!

Psalm 46:1-3

24

Prince of Peace. Mighty God. Father. Son. Holy Spirit. Comforter. Friend. Teacher. Provider. Holy One. Sustainer. Rock of Ages. The Great I Am. Alpha and Omega—the Beginning and the End. Companion. Leader. Lover of my soul. Great Physician and Healer.

Despised. Hated. Ridiculed. Spat upon. Beaten. Crucified.

In the darkest days, I am here. In the midst of pain and trouble, I am here. I am working. Through shattered lives and brokenness, I emerge victorious.

There is no problem too big, no hurt too deep, that I cannot overcome and bring healing. So bring it all to me, my child. Sit with me and let me hold you close. I bring grace and promise and hope and new life.

Leave the old behind—the hurts and anger, the failures, the pain. Leave it. Drop it and do not look back.

Go forth with me into a victorious future. Trust me with your all. Trust. Allow me to bring the peace and hope and grace and joy that you need, and be thankful.

I am able. I promise. Rejoice!

Isaiah 9:6-7

25

A day of rest—created for you and for me. When I created the world, I rested. Is that not reason enough for you, too, to rest? Celebrate my birth by resting your spirit.

Rest is essential to life. Why else do you have night and day? So rest, my children, and let my spirit soak into your very being. Become renewed and refreshed. Be ready again to serve me in my kingdom. I created you in my image. Follow my lead and my directives, and your life will be a blessing. I promise. Rejoice!

Exodus 16:30

26

When storms assail you, trust in me. Do not fret, but keep your eyes on me. I can help you weather any storm. I am able and can do all things. Dismiss worry and fear. Embrace my love and care and protection. It is enough for any situation. I promise. Rejoice!

Zechariah 9:14-15a

27

Help us, Lord, to be obedient, to be faith-filled, to be grateful.

You think I have deserted you, my child. You think I am nowhere to be found. You are unsure about the future, and you are angry with me. You try to let go, but instead, you grieve that you do not seem to be able to control the events of your life. You feel your days are cloudy and not filled with the sunshine of my presence.

You must wait. You must not lose hope. You must remember my faithfulness to you in the past. You must seek my peace. You must hold on to me at every turn. You must put aside all bitterness and anger and disappointment. You must stop your ceaseless efforts to make your life follow the path you deem right. When you can stop, then you must breathe in my name…breathe out my name. Trust me, for I have not left you alone. Believe in my plans for you, even when you have no idea what they are.

I am here. I promise. Rejoice!

I Peter 1:21; Hebrews 11:1

28

Loosen my strings, Lord—those strings of the need to control, the need for security, the fear of the unknown, the inability to be what everyone needs me to be. I need your help. I need you close. I need to trust and to believe that you are able.

I tell you, child, that I am near—at hand. Turn from fretting and from fear, and trust me. I am able to do *all* things. I promise. Rejoice!

Philippians 4:5-6; Matthew 4:17

29

The rains of my spirit fall on my children and nourish, cleanse and refresh you, even as the waters from the sky do the same for the earth.

This has been such a time for you, a time to rest in me, wait in my presence, commune with me. You are refreshed now, and I am actively answering your prayers. I am always with you—always at hand. Stay close to me in the days ahead. Stand amazed as you contemplate the many ways I am working in your lives.

You have been kind to my creatures, just as I am kind to you. And just like the nature you love and observe, take no worries with you into the days ahead. I am with you. I prepare the way before you. I promise. Rejoice!

Psalm 68:9; Romans 15:32-33

30

Letting go of the past is difficult, Lord—whether it be possessions or hurts.

The past is over, child, and the only sure thing you have is the present moment. Try to embrace each moment as it comes. Look for the opportunities inherent within each moment and allow my spirit to move and work through you. When you can do this, you will find that blessings will abound. I promise. Rejoice!

Ezekiel 36:27

31

Nourishing. Enriching. I am always aware of the needs in your life and in your spirit. Just as raindrops refresh the earth and promote new growth, so does the fresh dew of my spirit refresh your soul. When you spend time with me, dewdrops of my spirit fall on you, and you are renewed. Be not anxious about the future. Look forward with great anticipation, and take time each day to be renewed. Time spent with me, your father, will refresh you for the days ahead. I promise. Rejoice!

Jeremiah 31:25

How to Listen

TO GOD

The words and instructions following are extracted as a quote from the book, *How to Listen to God: Overcoming Addiction Through Practice of Two-Way Prayer* by Wally Paton, published by Faith With Works Publishing Company, Tucson, AZ, copyright 2000. At the end of his book, Mr. Paton uses an unpublished brochure by a gentleman named John Batterson ("How to Listen to God") to illustrate a method for listening to God. The brochure is copied in its entirety in hopes that you, too, might be able to learn to listen and hear God's instructions for you.*

*As a disclaimer, it seems that not everyone is able to follow Mr. Batterson's instructions and gain the results that they want. Let me quote a passage from the book *God Calling*, which was written by one of the "Two Listeners" who prayed together as this book was written. The section is titled "The Voice Divine." She relates the way she and a friend came to try listening to God, and this is what she says:

"My results were entirely negative. Portions of texts came and went; then my mind wandered to ordinary topics. I brought it back again and again, but with no success. To this day, I cannot get guidance in this way alone.

"But with my friend a very wonderful thing happened. From the first, beautiful messages were given to her by our Lord Himself, and every day from then these messages have never failed us."15

So you see, even one of the Two Listeners from *God Calling* did not achieve her goals in listening, but in praying together, this wonderful book came to be. God uses us all in ways of His own choosing. My prayer is that the words in this book will be a life guide for you! Blessings!

Carol Boseman Taylor
2015

How to Listen to God

These are a few simple suggestions for people who are willing to make an experiment. You can discover for yourself the most important and practical thing any human being can ever learn—how to be in touch with God.

All that is needed is the *willingness to try it honestly.* Every person who has done this consistently and sincerely has found that it really works.

Before you begin, look over these fundamental points. They are true and are based on the experience of thousands of people.

1. God is alive. He always has been and He always will be.

2. God knows everything.

3. God can do anything.

4. God can be everywhere—all at the same time. (These are the important differences between God and us human beings.)

5. God is invisible—we can't see Him or touch Him—but *God is here.* He is with you now. He is beside you. He surrounds you. He fills the room or the whole place where you are right now. He is in you now. He is in your heart.

6. God cares very much for *you.* He is interested in you. He has a plan for your life. He has an answer for every need and problem you face.

7. God will tell you all that you *need* to know. He will not always tell you all that you *want* to know.

8. God will help you do anything that He asks you to do.

9. Anyone can be in touch with God, anywhere and at any time, *if the conditions are obeyed.*

These are the conditions:
- To be quiet and still
- To listen
- To be honest about every thought that comes
- To test the thoughts to be sure that they come from God
- To obey

So, with these basic elements as a background, here are specific suggestions on how to listen to God:

1. *Take Time*
Find some place and time where you can be alone, quiet and undisturbed. Most people have found that the early morning is the best time. Have with you some paper and pen or pencil.

2. *Relax*
Sit in a comfortable position. Consciously relax all your muscles. Be loose. There is no hurry. There needs to be no strain during these minutes. God cannot get through to us if we are tense and anxious about later responsibilities.

3. *Tune In*
Open your heart to God. Either silently or aloud, just say to God in a natural way that you would like to find His plan for your life—you want His answer to the problem or situation that you are facing just now. Be definite and specific in your request.

4. *Listen*
Just be still, quiet, relaxed and open. Let your mind go "loose." Let God do the talking. Thoughts, ideas, and impressions will begin to come into your mind and heart. Be alert and aware and open to every one.

5. *Write!*
Here is the important key to the whole process. Write down everything that comes into your mind. *Everything*. Writing is simply a means of recording so that you can remember later. *Don't* sort out or edit your thoughts at this point.

Don't say to yourself:
> This thought isn't important;
> This is just an ordinary thought;
> This can't be guidance;
> This isn't nice;
> This can't be from God;
> This is just me thinking, etc.

Write down everything that passes through your mind:

Names of people;
Things to do;
Things to say;
Things that are wrong and need to be made right.

Write down everything:

Good thoughts—bad thoughts;
Comfortable thoughts—uncomfortable thoughts;
"Holy" thoughts—"unholy" thoughts;
Sensible thoughts—"crazy" thoughts.

Be honest! Write down *everything*. A thought comes quickly, and it escapes even more quickly unless it is captured and put down.

6. *Test*

When the flow of thoughts slows down, stop. Take a good look at what you have written. *Not every thought we have comes from God.* So we need to test our thoughts. Here is where the written record helps us to be able to look at them.

(a) Are these thoughts completely *honest, pure, unselfish and loving?*
(b) Are these thoughts in line with our duties to our family, to our country?
(c) Are these thoughts in line with our understanding of the teachings found in our spiritual literature?

7. *Check*

When in doubt and when it is important, what does another person who is living two-way prayer think about this thought or action? More light comes in through two windows than one. Someone else who also wants God's plan for our lives may help us to see more clearly.

Talk over together what you have written. Many people do this. They tell each other what guidance has come. This is the secret of unity. There are always three sides to every question—your side, my side, and the right side. Guidance shows us which is the right side—not who is right, but what is right.

8. *Obey*

Carry out the thoughts that have come. You will only be sure of guidance as you go through with it. A rudder will not guide a boat until the boat is moving. As you obey, very often the results will convince you that you are on the right track.

9. *Blocks?*

What if I don't seem to get any definite thoughts? God's guidance is as freely available as the air we breathe. If I am not receiving thoughts when I listen, the fault is not God's.

Usually it is because there is something *I will not do:*
> Something wrong in my life that I will not face and make right;
> A habit or indulgence I will not give up;
> A person I will not forgive;
> A wrong relationship in my life I will not give up;
> A restitution I will not make;
> Something God has already told me to do that I will not obey.

Check these points and be honest. Then try listening again.

10. *Mistakes*

Suppose I make a mistake and do something in the name of God that isn't right? Of course we make mistakes. We are humans with many faults. However, *God will always honor our sincerity.*

He will work around and through every honest mistake we make. He will help us make it right. *But remember this!* Sometimes when we do obey God, someone else may not like it or agree with it. So when there is opposition, it doesn't always mean you have made a mistake. It can mean that the other person doesn't want to know or to do what is right.

Suppose I fail to do something that I have been told and the opportunity to do it passes? There is only one thing to do. Put it right with God. Tell Him you're sorry. Ask Him to forgive you, then accept His forgiveness and begin again. God is our Father—He is not an impersonal calculator. He understands far better than we do.

11. *Results*

We never know what swimming is like until we get down into the water and try. We will never know what this is like until we sincerely try it.

Every person who has tried this honestly finds that a wisdom, not their own, comes into their minds and that Power greater than human power begins to operate in their lives. It is an endless adventure.

There is a way of life for everyone, everywhere. Anyone can be in touch with the living God, anywhere, anytime, *if we fulfill His conditions:*

> *When man listens, God Speaks.*
> *When man obeys, God Acts.*
>
> *This is the law of prayer.*

God's plan for this world goes forward through the lives of ordinary people who are willing to be governed by Him.

John E. Batterson[14]

[1] *The Hymnal for Worship & Celebration* (Word Music, Nashville, Tennessee, 1985), 66 (To God Be the Glory).

[2] Ibid., 411 (The Joy of the Lord)

[3] Ibid., 335 (Turn Your Eyes Upon Jesus)

[4] *Calvary Baptist Hymnal,* Words & Music by Mr. and Mrs. Seth Sykes, 1940, renewal 1968 by Seth Sykes, Assigned to Singspiration/ASCAP (Thank You, Lord)

[5] *The Hymnal for Worship & Celebration,* 4 (How Great Thou Art)

[6] Ibid., 428 (I Need Thee Every Hour)

[7] *How Majestic Is Your Name,* by Michael W. Smith, Copyright 1981 by Meadowgreen Music Co.

[8] *Blest Be The Tie That Binds,* lyrics by John Fawcet, 1782, Copyright: Public Domain, based on Hosea 11:4 and I Corinthians 12:25.

[9] *Turn Your Eyes Upon Jesus,* lyrics by Helen H. Lemmel, 1922, Copyright: Public Domain, based on Hebrews 12:2.

[10] *Surely the Presence of the Lord,* by Lanny Wolfe, 1977, Copyright 1977 by Lanny Wolfe Music. All rights controlled by Gaither Copyright Management.

[11] *The Hymnal for Worship & Celebration,* 624 (Doxology)

[12] Ibid., 345 (Blessed Assurance)

[13] Ibid., 428 (I Need Thee Every Hour)

[14] *How to Listen to God: Overcoming Addiction Through Practice of Two-Way Prayer,* 305-308 (*How to Listen to God,* by John E. Batterson, unpublished)

[15] *God Calling,* edited by A. J. Russell, "The Voice Divine," published by Barbour Publishing, Uhrichsville, OH 44683, copyright 1989 by Arthur James Ltd., Evesham, UK

CPSIA information can be obtained
at www.ICGtesting.com
Printed in the USA
FSHW021559170520
70263FS